D1514835

WHAT ARE HUMAN RIGHTS?

What are Human Rights?

MAURICE CRANSTON

TAPLINGER PUBLISHING CO., INC.

NEW YORK

First published in the United States in 1973 by
TAPLINGER PUBLISHING CO., INC.
New York, New York

Library of Congress Catalog Card Number: 73-4849

ISBN 0-8008-8148-6

CONTENTS

ACKNOWLEDGMENTS

Acknowledgments are due to the authorities of the United Nations and the Council of Europe for access to archives and for permission to reproduce documents. The author also wishes to record his gratitude to the Research Committee of the London School of Economics for its support and to Miss Catherine Hodges for her assistance.

This book is a revised and greatly extended version of an essay originally published in London as *Human Rights Today* (Ampersand Ltd., 1962) and in New York as *What are Human Rights?* (Basic Books, 1964).

I
What are Human Rights?

Human rights is a twentieth-century name for what has been traditionally known as natural rights or, in a more exhilarating phrase, the rights of man. Much has been said about them, and yet one may still be left wondering what they are. John Locke,[1] the philosopher most often quoted as an authority on the subject, wrote of the rights to life, liberty, and property. The Bill of Rights enacted by the English Parliament after the 'Glorious Revolution' in 1689—the same year in which Locke first published his theory of government—named also the right to trial by jury, and prescribed that in all courts of law excessive bail should not be required, nor excessive fines imposed, nor cruel and unusual punishments inflicted.

Locke's reasoning and the example of the English Bill of Rights had a great influence throughout the civilised world. In Virginia in June 1776, a Bill of Rights was adopted by a representative convention, and its first clause proclaimed 'that all men are by nature equally free and independent, and have certain inherent rights, of which, when they enter into a state of society, they cannot, by any compact, deprive or divest their posterity: namely, the enjoyment of life and liberty, with the means of acquiring and possessing property and pursuing and obtaining happiness'.

Here the right to happiness is added to those Locke named. The same word recurs in the Declaration of Independence issued by the thirteen American states in July 1776: 'We hold these truths to be self-evident: that all men are created equal; that they are endowed by their Creator with certain inalienable rights; that among these are life, liberty, and the pursuit of happiness.'

The United States Constitution of 1789, with concurrent amendments, defined these rights in greater detail. It specified

[1] See Notes, p. 168 et seq.

freedom of speech and the press, the 'right of the people to be secure in their persons, houses, papers, and effects against unreasonable searches and seizures'; and the right (which Locke, incidentally, denied to Roman Catholics) to the free exercise of religion. Nineteenth-century amendments made slavery illegal and also stated that 'the right of citizens of the United States to vote shall not be denied or abridged by the United States or by any State on account of race, colour, or previous condition of servitude'.

The Declaration of the Rights of Man and the Citizen issued by the Constituent Assembly in France follows closely the English and American models. It asserts that 'men are born and remain free and equal in rights', indeed that 'the purpose of all political association is the conservation of the natural and inalienable rights of man: these rights are liberty, property, security, and resistance to oppression'. In the same French Declaration liberty is defined as 'being unrestrained in doing anything that does not interfere with the liberty of another'. Besides property, which is held to be 'an inviolable and sacred right', the French Declaration specifies the right to free speech, a free press, religious freedom, and freedom from arbitrary arrest.

Such are the classical statements of the rights of man. Yet it would be a mistake to think of this notion as the child of the Enlightenment; it is much more ancient. Citizens of certain Greek cities enjoyed such rights as *isogoria*, or equal freedom of speech, and *isonomia*, or equality before the law, which are prominent among the rights claimed in the modern world. In the Hellenistic period which followed the breakdown of the Greek city-states, the Stoic philosophers formulated the doctrine of natural rights as something which belonged to all men at all times; these rights were not the particular privileges of citizens of particular cities, but something to which every human being everywhere was entitled, in virtue of the simple fact of being human and rational.

Locke was writing as a disciple of the Stoics when he offered his theory of natural rights to seventeenth-century readers who were troubled by the collapse of the traditional political order and forced to think out anew the nature of their duties and rights. The notion of natural rights has continued to attract men's minds; and the constitutions or the legal codes of practically every state in the world today give at least formal recognition to 'the rights of man and the citizen'.

Sweden in 1809 and Holland in 1815 followed the English model of incorporating the concept of natural rights into the constitution of a monarchy; other nations copied the American model of a republic having the preservation of men's natural rights as its declared *raison d'être*. When the United Nations was created after the Second World War, one of the first and most important tasks assigned to it was what Winston Churchill called 'the enthronement of human rights'.

And yet the theory of natural rights has never gone unchallenged, even in the times of its greatest popularity. Among the mandarins of English political philosophy, Hume, Burke, Bentham, Austin, most Hegelian Idealists of the nineteenth century, and positivists of the twentieth have been opposed to the doctrine. Some Idealist philosophers admitted a concept of rights, but went on to argue that rights belonged not to individuals but to societies or communities. In Germany especially the Idealist influence was strong. The Declaration of Rights proclaimed by the nationalist German liberals in 1848 was no longer individualist; whereas the American and French declarations had asserted the rights of *man*, the German manifesto spoke instead of 'the rights *of the German people*'.

The English Idealist philosopher F. H. Bradley wrote in 1894:

'The rights of the individual are today not worth serious criticism . . . The welfare of the community is the end and is the ultimate standard. And over its members the right of its moral organism is absolute. Its duty and its right is to dispose of these members as it seems best.'

In the realm of ideology both nationalism and Communism are inclined to this same conclusion. Marx regarded the notion of the rights of man as a bourgeois illusion; he was hostile to the individualism which underlies the classical doctrine or rights. Marx believed in humanity, in man as a 'species being', and he argued that this humanity would come into its own only when men ceased to think of themselves in bourgeois terms as individuals with separate inalienable rights.

In spite of Marx's teaching on this subject, the Soviet Union, in its constitution of 1936 with amendments to 1965, formulated the rights of its citizens on the model of the constitutions of America and France and other 'bourgeois' countries. For example, according to Article 125 of the Soviet Constitution: 'Citizens of the U.S.S.R. are guaranteed by law (a) freedom of speech; (b) freedom of the press; (c) freedom of assembly, including the holding of mass meetings; (d) freedom of street processions and demonstrations.'

Leaving aside, for the moment, the question of what these 'constitutional guarantees' are worth, it is interesting to note that even in the darkest days of Stalinism, the Soviet leaders felt it necessary to give nominal recognition to the notions of rights. The very fact that they have been written into Communist as well as other constitutions is itself an important sign, for it shows that however difficult it may be to explain the idea of human rights, that idea has somehow acquired almost universal assent.

But we are still left with the question of explanation. What does it mean to say that all men have rights? Manifestly, the word 'right' is ambiguous. First, there is a sense in which to have a right is to have something which is conceded and enforced by the law of the realm. To say that I have a right to leave the country, a right to vote in parliamentary elections, a right to bequeath my estate to anyone I choose, is to say that I live under a government which allows me to do these things, and will come to my aid if anyone tries to stop me.

'Right' in this sense is not the same as desert. For example, nationals of some British Commonwealth countries living in England have felt aggrieved because they are not allowed to vote in parliamentary elections in the United Kingdom while citizens of the Irish Republic, which is not even a member of the Commonwealth, do have this right. It is a right enjoyed by Irish citizens even if they pay no taxes, and one denied to some Commonwealth nationals, no matter how much tax they pay to the British government, and no matter how long they have lived in the British Isles. From the point of view of deserts, and of justice, there is certainly something odd about a situation where people who both reside permanently in Great Britain and pay taxes to the British exchequer should be denied a right which is granted to Irish people who commonly repudiate any allegiance to the British throne and do not necessarily pay British taxes. Unjust this may be, but that makes no difference to the fact that this right *exists*. Irishmen are entitled by English law to vote in English elections. Their right is a verifiable reality.

Rights of this kind I shall speak of henceforth as *positive* rights. What is characteristic of them is that they are recognised by positive law, the actual law of actual states. There is, however, a second sense of the word 'right' which is different from positive right, and much closer to the idea of deserts or justice. Suppose the father of a family says, 'I have a right to know what is going on in my own house.' He is not saying anything about his position under positive law; he is not saying that the courts of justice will ensure that he is kept informed of what happens in his house. He is not so much making a statement of fact as making a special kind of claim. He is appealing to the principle that being the head of a house gives a man a just title to expect to be told what goes on in it. The right he speaks of is a *moral* right.

There is a considerable difference between a right in the sense of a positive right and a right in the sense of a moral right. First, a positive right is necessarily enforceable; if it is not enforced, it cannot be a positive right. A moral right is not necessarily enforced. Some moral rights are enforced and some are not. To say, for instance, that I have a moral right to receive a decent salary is not to say that I *do* receive one. On the contrary, it is far more probable that the man who says, 'I've a right to receive a decent salary' is the man who thinks his salary is not what it should be. Immanuel Kant once said that we are most keenly aware of a moral duty when it is at variance with what we wish, or feel inclined, to do. In the same way we are most acutely conscious of a moral right when it is *not* being conceded.

There is another feature which distinguishes moral rights from positive rights. We can find out what our positive rights are by reading the laws that have been enacted, looking up law books, or going to court and asking a judge. There is no similar authority to consult about our moral rights. You may think you have a moral right to something, and someone else may think you have not; but there is nothing you can do to prove that you have a moral right, and nothing your critic can do to prove that you have not. What you can do is to try to *justify* your claim, and your critic can try to *justify* his criticisms. But justification is a very different thing from proof and from obtaining an authoritative ruling from some institution of positive law.

These considerations point to the first question that must be asked about human rights. Are they some kind of positive right or some kind of moral right, something men actually have or something men ought to have? Let us take a particular example. According to Article 13 of the Universal Declaration of Human Rights which was 'proclaimed' by the United Nations in 1948, 'Everyone has the right to leave any country, including his own, and return to his country.' If this is read as a statement of fact, it is simply not true. An Englishman, like myself, is assuredly free to leave his country and return to it unless he is detained by order of a court of law. The same situation prevails in many other countries, but not in all. Even in the United States, several American citizens have had their passports impounded by the government; in South Africa passports are commonly denied to black Africans; and in Russia relatively few passports are ever issued at all. Clearly, therefore, the right to leave any country, which the United Nations Declaration says 'everyone' has, is not a positive right. The intention of the sponsors of that declaration was to specify something that everyone *ought* to have. In other words the rights they named were moral rights.

To say that human rights are moral rights is not to deny that they are for many people positive rights as well as moral rights. Where human rights are upheld by positive law—where people have what they ought to have—human rights are both moral rights and positive rights. But it is essential to keep in mind the distinction between what is and what ought to be, between the empirical and the normative, between the realm of fact and that of morality. I do not share the belief of those philosophers who claim that these two realms are totally distinct and impenetrable. But we cannot understand how the empirical and

6

the normative are sometimes united unless we first recognise the difference between them.

In classifying human rights as moral rights it is important to notice something which distinguishes them from other kinds of moral right. This is that they are *universal*. Many of the moral rights that we speak of belong to particular people because they are in particular situations: the rights of a landowner, for example, or the rights of an editor, or a clergyman, or a judge, or a stationmaster. These men's special rights arise from their special positions and are intimately linked with their duties. But human rights are not rights which derive from a particular station; they are rights which belong to a man simply because he is a man. In the words of Jacques Maritain:

> 'The human person possesses rights because of the very fact that it is a person, a whole, master of itself and of its acts, and which consequently is not merely a means to an end, but an end, an end which must be treated as such. The dignity of the human person? The expression means nothing if it does not signify that by virtue of natural law, the human person has the right to be respected, is the subject of rights, possesses rights. These are things which are owed to man because of the very fact that he is man.'[2]

Jacques Maritain writes with eloquence, but whether one can accept his argument or not depends on one's attitude to the crucial concept he invokes: that of natural law. One cannot speak for long about the rights of man without confronting this notion, for it is customary to say that just as positive rights are rooted in positive law, natural rights—or human rights—are rooted in natural law. The validity of the one depends on the validity of the other. I shall therefore attempt in my next chapter to look a little more closely at the credentials of natural law.

II
Rights and Morality

It is a very ancient notion that there is a law which is different from the law of earthly rulers—different from, and also higher and more compelling than, the edicts of courts or princes. One of the earliest and most eloquent expressions of this thought is given by Sophocles, in his play *Antigone*. Readers will remember that Creon, King of Thebes, has decreed that Polynices, a traitor who has been killed in the field, shall be left unburied, his body exposed to the vultures and the dogs. Antigone, the sister of Polynices, rebels against this ruling, because, she claims, every man has a right to burial. 'And what right has the King', she demands, 'to keep me from my own brother?' Antigone buries the corpse, is discovered, arrested, and taken to Creon.

'Do you know the law?' the King asks her.

'Yes,' she replies.

'Then why did you break it?'

Antigone answers that the edict she has disobeyed is not sanctioned by conscience; it may be the law of the state, but it is contrary to the law of justice:

> Nor did I deem that thou, a mortal man,
> Could'st by a breath annul and override
> The immutable, unwritten laws of heaven:
> They were not born today nor yesterday;
> They die not, and none knoweth whence they sprang.

Creon replies that Polynices was a traitor and that no ruler can let traitors go unpunished. A state must have laws and uphold them. The ruler must be obeyed in all things, just and unjust alike, or the result will be anarchy. 'And what evil', Creon asks, 'is worse than anarchy?'

Sophocles would not have written as good a play as he did if he had not made the case for Creon as strong, in its way, as he made the case for Antigone. Drama—and history—yield many examples of subjects with far better causes than Antigone's in conflict with rulers with far worse causes than Creon's. The merit of Sophocles' play is that it simplifies nothing. It shows what a serious and terrible thing it is to defy that positive law by which the safety of society is secured, to rebel against established authority in the name of conscience or 'the immutable, unwritten laws of heaven'.

Sophocles, after all, was a statesman and a general as well as a poet. Moreover, he was a conservative in politics, and his sympathies were with Antigone largely because he wished to preserve the authority of traditional religious belief against the progressive notion that might is right. Sophocles was certainly not a liberal, and yet he was clearly on the side of Antigone against Creon. He wrote to win the public's sympathy for what she says and does. Creon argues that 'the state must be obeyed in all things—*just and unjust alike*'. Antigone's claim is that the state need not be obeyed if what it commands is wrong. Sophocles is with her. He believes, as she does, that the unwritten law of heaven is superior to the law of the state. The rights Antigone claims are rights bestowed by the higher law, so that positive law cannot take them from her.

It is easy to respond emotionally to Sophocles' play, but whether one can accept his argument depends finally on whether one agrees with him that there is a law which is higher than positive law. For Sophocles, and for many generations of Christians who also believed in the existence of a law higher than man-made law, there was no difficulty about naming the source of this higher law: it was the supreme being in heaven. But is it essential to have a conception of the deity in order to justify belief in the existence of natural law?

Philosophers and jurists have been reluctant to surrender the whole issue to theologians. The most popular answer among philosophers and jurists to the question, 'What is the law which is higher than positive law?' has been 'natural law'. This concept of natural law, though foreshadowed by Sophocles and to some extent by Aristotle, was first elaborated, together with the concept of natural rights, by the Stoics of the Hellenistic period. Natural law for them embodied those elementary principles of justice which were apparent, they believed, to the 'eye of reason' alone. The Stoics of Rome, though jurists rather than philosophers, upheld the same idea. Cicero said, 'There is a true law, right reason, in accordance with nature; it is unalterable and eternal.'

The political theory of medieval Christendom put even greater stress on natural law, which was understood as being part of the law of God; and it was only after the Renaissance that natural law was restated in secular, modern, individualist terms by such theorists as Grotius and Pufendorf and Locke. This is not to say that Cicero and St Thomas Aquinas and Locke all understood natural law in exactly the same way.[1] We may doubt, for example, that Cicero or St Thomas thought of natural law as something which bestowed the right of rebellion in the way that some of the Greeks did or that Locke did. Yet the idea of natural law as a universal moral law which transcends the law of states is one by which European thinking about politics has been permeated for more than two thousand years. And although it went out of fashion in the nineteenth century, it has come into favour again since the Second World War. At Nuremberg in 1945, natural law was freely invoked as the legal basis of at least some of the elements of the indictment of the Nazi leaders.

Natural law is thus a living as well as an ancient concept. It might nevertheless be a fallacious one. There is certainly something suspicious about the things which are said by many champions of natural law. Consider, for example, a remark from the writings of the eighteenth-century jurist William Blackstone: 'Natural law is binding all over the globe; no human laws have any validity if contrary to it.' Now if the word 'valid' means what it commonly means for lawyers, this statement is simply untrue. For by a valid law, lawyers commonly mean a law which is actually upheld and enforced by the courts, a law which is pronounced valid by a duly established judge. A great many laws contrary to natural law were upheld by courts in different parts of the globe in the eighteenth century when Blackstone wrote those words. For instance, there were the laws which authorised slavery, an institution which Blackstone himself regarded as being contrary to natural law. Laws even more at odds with natural law were upheld by duly constituted courts in Germany at the time of the Third Reich. Thus, in the usual lawyers' sense of the word 'valid', some positive laws which are contrary to natural law *are* valid; if this is what Blackstone was denying, then his assertion was false.

The truth of the matter, however, is that Blackstone was trying to say something else. He was thinking of a kind of validity which is different from validity in the ordinary legal sense. He meant that any positive law which was contrary to natural law had no validity *in conscience*; he meant that such a law was not *morally* compelling and had no *just* title to obedience. But Blackstone failed to make this point as he might and should have made it. He failed to discriminate clearly between what is and what ought to be.

Locke is in some ways an even more unsatisfactory exponent of natural law. In his Latin *Essays on the Law of Nature*,[2] Locke argues that because the study of the universe shows that laws are operating throughout nature, it follows that there must be laws governing the conduct of men. Locke does not mean psychological laws; he means moral laws, the sort of laws embodied in natural law. Science, says Locke, shows that laws are universally operative. Therefore, he concludes, science demonstrates the existence of natural law.

This is a bad argument. For the laws discovered in nature by scientists are not laws in the sense in which moralists and lawyers speak of laws. A scientific law is an observed regularity in nature, and it embodies a kind of prediction. It is not something which can be obeyed or disobeyed at will. If something happened which was contrary to an established scientific law, that scientific law would no longer be a scientific law; it would become a discredited, outmoded, forsaken scientific hypothesis. A law of conduct, on the other hand, can be obeyed or disobeyed; and it certainly does not cease to be a moral law if someone breaks it.

Locke's argument is an attempt to derive a conclusion about law in the sense of moral law from a true statement about law in the sense of scientific law; it rests on a mistake of logic. In fairness, however, it must be said that this is not peculiar to Locke. It is a lucid statement of one of the standard traditional arguments for the existence of natural law.

This sort of mistake has prompted some theorists to argue that the whole idea of natural law is a form of bogus metaphysics rooted in confusion of language. Bentham was of this opinion; or perhaps one should say Bentham *is* of this opinion, for his body, embalmed and dressed in the clothes of 1831, still sits in a little cabinet in the hall of University College, London. At any rate, he wrote in *Anarchical Fallacies*: 'Right is a child of law; from real laws come real rights, but from imaginary law, from "laws of nature", come imaginary rights . . . Natural rights is simple nonsense; natural and imprescriptible rights (an American phrase) rhetorical nonsense, nonsense upon stilts.'

Bentham is here stating in picturesque language the central tenet of legal positivism—namely, that positive law alone is real law and that natural law is not law at all. Legal theorists since the eighteenth century have tended to attach themselves to one of two schools: the school of natural law or the school of legal positivism. The arguments of positivism are brisker, and perhaps more readily convincing than those of the champions of natural law; but they lack subtlety. There is something arbitrary and dictatorial about the positivist assertion that there is only one genuine kind of law.

Clearly, natural law is not law in the same sense in which positive law is law. Positive law is a collection of specific enactments, with definite sanctions attached to many of them. Natural law is not written down and carries no specific sanctions. But this does not mean, as the positivists claim, that it is unreal, imaginary, fallacious, or meaningless. It can be regarded as such only if one insists that all law shall be like positive law. But this demand is intolerably high-handed and dogmatic. The English language allows for a very much freer use of the word 'law'. Natural law is entitled to the name law because it is *authoritative*, something which can be obeyed or disobeyed. This is not to say that the principles of natural law are in any crude sense imperatives. But neither are the laws contained in positive law. Professor Gilbert Ryle has written (although in another connection):

> 'Ethical statements, as distinct from particular *ad hominem* behests and reproaches, should be regarded as warrants addressed to any potential givers of behests and reproaches; i.e. not as personal action-tickets but as

impersonal injunction-tickets; not imperatives but "laws", that only such things as imperatives and punishments can satisfy. Like statute laws they are to be construed not as orders, but as licences to give and enforce orders.'[3]

Moral laws are in some respects like positive laws, in other respects unlike them. The differences are extremely important. But the resemblance is important too, and the word 'law' is as properly employed in the case of natural law as in the case of positive law. Each kind of law has its own authority: positive law the authority of force, natural law the authority of justice or morality; and when positive law coincides with natural law it has the authority both of force and of justice. The test of validity, the criterion of authenticity, is different in each case. The answer to the question, 'Is so-and-so right?' depends, if it is a positive right, on whether it is *enforced*. If it is a natural right or human right which is in question, the answer depends on whether it is demanded by *justice*. Positive law secures the enforcement of positive rights; natural law gives the justice to natural rights.

Bentham's hostility to natural rights and natural law was not only due to his belief that they were unreal metaphysical entities; he also believed—and it was this which made him so impassioned—that talk about natural rights was mischievous. This attitude was shared by certain other critics of natural rights, such as David Hume and Edmund Burke.

This at first seems rather odd, since Bentham's general political outlook was entirely opposed to that of Hume and Burke. The explanation is that they apprehended different kinds of mischief. Bentham, a radical, objected to proclamations of natural rights because he thought that they took the place of ordinary and effective legislation. His argument was that governments which issued declarations of the rights of man were merely making rhetorical utterances which cost them nothing, instead of getting on with the real work of reform. Hume and Burke, on the other hand, were conservatives who disliked talk about the rights of man because it inflamed the common people to revolutionary action. It led men to think they were entitled to have things which they could not possibly have.

Burke, in his *Reflections on the Revolution in France*, asserts that the sponsors of the French Declaration of the Rights of Man have done great social harm by proclaiming what he calls the 'monstrous fiction' of human equality. Natural differences between men are so great, he argues, that equality is an impossible objective. And to set forth this fiction as if it were a reality is to inspire 'false ideas and vain expectations into men destined to travel in the obscure walk of laborious life' and 'to aggravate and embitter that real inequality which it never can remove'.[4]

All these criticisms of natural rights have assuredly some force in them. There has undoubtedly been a connection, as the conservative critics say, between propaganda for the rights of man and much revolutionary action in the modern world, not only in the case of such successful revolutions as the English Revolution of 1688, the American Revolution, and the Great Revolution in France, but equally in the case of revolutionary movements which have been less favoured by fortune. Undoubtedly also, in our own time, which has been characterised by so many revolts against alien rule or colonialism, easy talk about human rights has inspired in Burke's words, 'false ideas and vain expectations' among the inhabitants of many undeveloped places.

Bentham's complaint about declarations of metaphysical rights being a wretched substitute for the enactment of positive law has also a close relevance to the problems of the present day. One can well imagine that a Czech or a South African who has had his passport impounded by his government might find it particularly irritating to read in the Universal Declaration of Human Rights that 'everyone has the right to leave any country, including his own . . .' If he is denied the positive right, of what use is it to him to be told that he has this human right, this moral right? What he wants is deeds, not words. And that, in the end, is what not only he and Bentham but all of us want. Even so, I think we should not follow Bentham in being so readily contemptuous of words. It *is* of some use to the man who is refused the right to leave his country that the world should formally recognise his moral right to do so. Indeed, such a man can only protest as he does insofar as he can make people understand that a *wrong* is being done to him, that something he ought to have is being denied him. He may dislike being confined within the borders of one republic, but he cannot claim that it is *wrong* that he should be so confined without appealing to some general or universal principle that no man ought to be so confined—without invoking, in other words, the moral right of everyone 'to leave any country, including his own'.

Whatever the 'mischief' done by talk of the rights of man, we must also remember that harmful social consequences can be attributed to the influence of legal positivism. Most positivist jurists, in saying that natural law is not law at all, have intended to say no more than that positive law is the only law which it is worth the while of lawyers to think about. However, the dissemination of the idea that positive law is the only law which it is worth the while of lawyers to think about has encouraged the belief that positive law is the only law which it is worth the while of *anyone* to think about. What is worse, it has encouraged the belief that positive law, being the only genuine law, is the only law which should be *obeyed*. The most sensational consequences of this line of thinking were to be observed in Germany under Hitler. There the edicts of the Nazi state were defined and enforced by men who sat on the bench and wore the robes of judges, so that the great mass of German people did not doubt that those edicts were lawful, and therefore required obedience. The voice of an Antigone was but seldom heard among them; and this was conceivably in some part due to the influence of positivism in German jurisprudence; for the doctrine of legal positivism is in effect identical with that of Creon, that law is nothing other than the command of a puissant sovereign.

Legal positivism encourages these attitudes, but in fairness one must add that it does not teach them. The primary objective of legal positivism is to distinguish positive law from morality. In defining law as it does, in making us conscious of what positive law is, legal positivism might also serve to make us more conscious of what morality is. It pushes morality out of the domain of jurisprudence; it says that moral philosophy is no part of the particular professional concern of the lawyer; but it does not deny that it is part of the general concern of ordinary men.

Indeed the legal positivists and the champions of natural law have one great thing in common: they are both acutely conscious of the great difference that exists between positive law and morality. It is after they have recognised the distinction that they part company, the theorists of natural law maintaining that morality is still part of law, and an essential part, the positivists wishing to remove it from law to the realm of moral philosophy.

Since it is as a political theorist and not as a lawyer that I have ventured to write these pages, I cannot decently quarrel with the positivists about the classification of natural law. But I believe that the use of philosophical reflection can itself serve to show that the champions of natural law were not so far wrong, after all. For the more one studies the use of the word 'law' among English-speaking peoples, the more one comes to realise that morality is, so to speak, built into its meaning. For although we must agree with the positivist that enforcement rather than justice is the necessary condition of a positive law being a positive law, one cannot talk for long about law without having entered, perhaps imperceptibly, the realm of value. The word 'law' in its most frequent uses is a normative word; its definition is intimately linked with the word 'justice' which is a normative word in all its uses. The word 'law' is defined as a system of justice, and justice, according to the first definition given in the Oxford Dictionary, is 'just conduct; fairness; the exercise of authority or power in maintenance of right'. This is not to say that all laws are just—far from it; but in looking at law we are looking for justice.

Having recognised the crucial distinction between the empirical and the normative, between the positive and the moral, we have to pass on to a further stage of awareness: that of recognising how the two are interwoven in the very language that we use. We cannot give a complete account of what we mean by law in terms of facts alone.

III
The Justification of Rights

There is a natural temptation to agree with Bentham's suggestion that natural rights is nonsense, but it is a temptation to which one should not too readily succumb. For when we speak of a right we are not simply talking about the facts of a positive legal system, and it is a distortion of language to pretend that we do. The word 'right', in ordinary English usage, not only means a 'lawful entitlement', it also means a 'just entitlement'. We all of us speak of our moral rights as well as legal or positive rights. Perhaps the most common use of the word 'right' is to make a claim and to assert, in making that claim, that one is morally entitled to do so. Just as a positive right belongs, by definition, to the realm of fact, of what *is*, so a moral right belongs, by definition, to the category of what *ought to be*. If Bentham's dictum is accepted, we should never be allowed to use the word 'right' in this second sense of a just entitlement. And why should we allow Bentham to rob us of a very important concept? Why should we seek to deny the ambiguity of a word and permit only one of its traditional and accepted uses?

The word 'rights' is used in more than one sense; and the time has now come to consider what those senses are. We have already noted the distinction between human rights and positive rights; I propose now to re-arrange rights into two other categories, the one I shall call legal rights, the other moral rights.

(1) *Legal rights* may be distinguished as follows:

(*a*) *General positive rights*: the rights that are enjoyed and fully assured to everyone living under a given jurisdiction or constitution.

(*b*) *Traditional rights and liberties*: Burke said that the English people had risen against James II because he had taken away their traditional rights and liberties as Englishmen. The Vichy government took away many of the traditional rights and liberties of Frenchmen. This class of rights includes lost positive rights as well as existing positive rights.

(c) *Nominal 'legal' rights*: Even the least liberal nations tend to have 'façade' constitutions[1] which 'guarantee' freedom of speech, movement, assembly, and other such rights to their inhabitants. But where these nominal rights are not enforced, they cannot, of course, be classed as positive rights. We nevertheless see the demand in some such places for the nominal 'legal' rights being made positive rights. One example is the demand of certain Polish intellectuals for that freedom of expression which their constitution assures them. An even more publicised example is the demand of the black Americans in the United States for the nominal legal right to vote, or to enter the same educational institutions as the white Americans, to be translated into positive rights.

(d) *Positive rights, liberties, privileges, and immunities of a limited class of persons*: Under this category we should have to include all rights which are attached to membership of a given category, e.g., the rights of clergymen, of peers, of doctors, ratepayers and so forth. The twentieth century has become impatient of privileges, and rights which were once enjoyed by a limited class of persons are often now claimed by all the inhabitants of a country. For example, the privileges of citizenship, the rights of ratepayers, as they were known in nineteenth-century England, are now enjoyed by all adult British subjects. A demand for the extension of rights within a political society is often confused with the demand for human rights. But the two are quite distinct.

(e) *The positive rights, liberties, privileges, and immunities of a single person*: Here the rights of the President of the United States, the rights of the King of England or the Lord Chancellor, or the Archbishop of Canterbury, are examples. Sometimes these rights come into collision with one another, as they did in seventeenth-century England.

The foregoing classes cover the category of legal rights. Next in turn is the category of moral rights. In this case it will be convenient to revise the order of generality.

(2) *Moral rights*

(*a*) *Moral rights of one person only*: We may adapt Bradley's phrase 'my station and its duties' and speak of 'my station and its rights'. I, and I alone, have a network of rights which arise from the fact that I have done certain deeds, paid certain monies, been elected to certain places, and so forth. Some of these rights are legal rights as well as moral rights. But in considering them as moral rights the question is not 'Does the law uphold them?' but 'Have I just claim to them?'. Not all my moral rights may be enjoyed. I have said that we become most conscious of our moral rights precisely when they are *not* upheld. I am inclined to say 'I have a moral right to be told what is going on in my own house' when I realise I am not being told. So just as the crucial question with legal rights is 'Are they secured and enjoyed?', the crucial question in a moral right is 'Is there a just title?'. Is there a sound moral claim? *Justification* is what is called for.

(*b*) *The moral rights of anyone in a particular situation*: This is the class of moral rights which belong to everyone who comes into a certain specific category: e.g., that of a parent, or a tutor, or an *au pair* girl. So we can say of a person, if he is a member of this class, he is entitled to so and so. Claims to have such moral rights are pressed by proving that one does belong to the appropriate category.

(*c*) *The moral right of all people in all situations*: Because these rights are universal we should naturally expect them to be few in number; and we should expect them to be highly generalised in their formulation. It is easier to agree, for example, about the kind of deed which violates the right to life than it is to agree about any philosophical expression of the right to life. Moreover, it is inevitable that such a right as that to liberty will be somewhat differently understood in different societies, where the boundary between liberty and licence will be differently drawn. Again, our understanding of the right to property will differ according to the meaning we give to that word.

The place which human rights occupy in my classification is readily understood. Human rights are a form of moral right, and they differ from other moral rights in being the rights of all people at all times and in all situations. This universal characteristic of human rights is a large part of our problem in seeking to justify them.

The kind of moral right which is the easiest to justify is the right of one person only. I, for example, claim a series of moral rights, and if called upon to justify these claims, I shall put forward one of the following arguments:

(1) I may say that I have *earned* the right. If I have composed a song, I claim the moral right to impose conditions on the publication of it. I have acquired that right by the creative labour of composition.

(2) I may say that I have *bought* the right. If I am a publisher, and have acquired, in a fair bargain, your authority to publish your song, then I have the moral right to publish it on the terms stipulated in the contract. Buying, of course, is an exercise that depends on the existence of money; but even in a society where money was unknown, it would still be possible to acquire moral rights by barter or some other form of contract analogous to buying. Promises, or contracts, create moral rights at the same time as they institute duties.

(3) I may say I have been *given* the right. This depends, of course on a giver having the right of ownership in what he bestows, but provided this condition is satisfied, a deliberate gift confers a perfect title on the recipient. If my wife has given me a watch, I have a just entitlement to possession of it.

(4) I may say I have *inherited* the right. This is a form of right which depends on the existence of a type of society where inheritance is a customary institution. But in all societies where fathers are expected to be breadwinners, a widow and a young child could reasonably claim a just entitlement to inherit a certain share of the estate of a dead man, on the grounds that in marriage a man acquires a contractual duty towards his wife to nourish her and her children, and this gives the wife the right to expect, with her children, to be nourished from his estate if he dies before she does.

In short, we justify the moral rights of an individual by arguing that those rights have been earned or that they have been acquired by gift, bequest, sale or some other contractual undertaking.

Besides the moral rights of one particular individual, there are, as we have seen, moral rights belonging to given classes of persons, such as parents, doctors, and priests. Many of the special rights of these classes of persons are set out in positive law and are therefore positive rights, but I am here concerned with their moral rights (which may or may not be positive rights), and the justification of these moral rights. This is sometimes expressed in the language of rôles. If a man enacts a certain rôle he acquires certain rights. For example, if a man becomes Archbishop of Canterbury, he acquires certain moral rights which derive from the rôle. He may claim, for example, the moral right to be consulted by the King of England about the matrimonial arrangements of the royal family. No other person, except the person who enacts the rôle of Prime Minister, has this same moral right. So here we have three people with moral rights and moral duties which flow from the rôles they perform. Performing the rôle of King of England obliges—or establishes the duty—for one man to tell the Archbishop of Canterbury and the Prime Minister about his matrimonial plans: performing the rôles of Archbishop and Prime Minister gives the other two men the moral right to enquire into the King's intentions. Since performing a rôle is largely a matter of discharging a set of duties, a man acquires the moral rights largely to the extent that he does the duties which the rôle imposes. A negligent or lazy Archbishop of Canterbury might well be said to forgo some (though scarcely all) of his moral rights. In this way, it would seem that the rights that derive from rôles are for the most part earned rights, or closely analogous to earned rights, as well as being exclusive rights, or rights that not everybody has.

One great difficulty in the justification of natural rights or human rights is that while they clearly belong to the category of moral rights they cannot be justified by the type of arguments we commonly use to justify the moral rights of the kinds I have so far considered. A human right is something that pertains to all men at all times. Therefore it cannot be justified in the way we justify rights that are earned or are acquired by the enactment of special rôles: human rights are not bought, nor are they created by any other specific contractual undertaking. They are not exclusive, they do not 'go with the job'. They are said to belong to man simply because he is a man. We must therefore turn next to examine the several rights which are said to be men's natural rights, and consider how each in turn might be justified, following the sequence set down by Locke of life, liberty, property.

IV

The Right to Life

The best justification for man's natural right to life is still perhaps Hobbes's argument. Natural rights begin as a claim which everyone naturally makes. Nobody wants to die a violent death, or to suffer an injury. These aversions are so universally and so intensely felt that we speak of them as natural. Man has a natural desire to survive, a natural impulse to defend himself from death and injury. Man is a being who is exceedingly vulnerable. His natural powers are not adequate for his own protection. Unlike lobsters and porcupines, *homo sapiens* has no defences in the structure of his own body. As Hobbes reminded us, the strongest man on earth can easily be killed while he is asleep.

Hobbes is sometimes unfairly accused of suggesting that man's desire to stay alive is the greatest of all his desires: in fact, Hobbes said that a man's pride could sometimes be more compelling than his fear of death: but at all events, there is no denying that the desire to stay alive is, generally speaking, man's paramount wish, and the one that demands from others their most unfailing respect. To say that man has a right to life is to convert that demand into a kind of moral imperative, that is, to impose on all men a reciprocal duty to abstain from injuring their neighbours.

Hobbes believed that the basis of all human societies was a form of non-aggression pact between beings whose only natural defence is aggression, and who did not relish the hazards of endless war. This was Hobbes's conception of the origin of law among men. He saw men as beings endowed with a power of reason which enables them to understand that in a community of persons where no one can defend himself effectively, the only safety lies in each member undertaking not to attack his neighbour on condition that his neighbour undertakes not to attack him. Institutions of law enforcement which can survive the deaths of any victim of aggression to punish the aggressor, serve to ensure, by a monopoly of supreme force, that the peace is kept.

The social contract, whether in Hobbes's or in any other formulation, is a myth: but it throws a certain light on the realities of the human condition. Men are not like ants and bees. Their impulses do not make them each do instinctively what is most useful to the community to have done. Each man has his own ideas as to what is best for himself and for others. And since collisions are therefore unavoidable, communities of men must have rules. Man, it has been said, is 'a rule-following animal'. The only way human beings can live in societies is to live according to rules. Indeed the very idea of a society can be understood only in terms of the recognition of rules. A society is not a mass, or crowd, or series; it is a group of persons, each related to the others by a shared adherence to a set of rules; there can be no society without some sort of regulations, any more than there can be a language or a game without rules.

Every particular society is likely to have its own distinctive rules, some more complex than others, but there is one rule which every society must have, and that is that no man shall use violence against the life and person of his neighbour (except in some special circumstances such as self-defence). Even in such societies as Sparta and the Third Reich where the assassination of certain minorities is permitted in certain seasons, the violence must be regulated by law. One citizen is not free to injure another; and the minorities may be killed only because they are *not* regarded as members of the society, and are often regarded as its enemies. Even the most odious types of human society must recognise the right to life of those people who are considered to be both loyal and fully human.

Rousseau once suggested that morality begins with human society; and at all events, man's awareness of morality is something he owes to the experience of living in society. In society, man can not only make a claim: he can assert that he is *entitled* to make that claim: he can justify his claim: he can use the language of rights. He can say not only that he does not want to be killed or injured, but that he *ought* not to be killed or injured, on the grounds that society as such must entail an understanding that peaceable man will be left in peace, and that everyone is entitled not to be injured so long as he does not injure anyone else. Society creates at the same time the duty not to injure one's neighbour and the right not to be injured by one's neighbour.

To say that all men have a right to life is to say that all men, who naturally attach paramount importance to survival, can claim to be left in peace and are entitled to have that claim recognised. But the question may well be asked: Is it natural to respect the natural desire to survive? All history and experience shows that men are killed, and have been killed in vast numbers by other men. The interesting thing, however, is that in every case, some kind of excuse or extenuating circumstances are pleaded. Let us consider the various types of situation in which men have been put to death:

(1) *Capital punishment.* The execution of murderers is obviously a deliberate act of killing, and yet it can be, and often is presented as an affirmation of the right to life; the argument being that the killer has forfeited his own right to life by denying another man's right to life; and that justice requires a penalty in kind. Modern opinion is increasingly opposed to this reasoning, but some of the greatest moral philosophers, including Kant, believed in it, and there is certainly nothing incongruous in the champion of capital punishment asserting the sanctity of the right to life. The case for non-capital punishment (which I myself favour) differs from the Kantian case, not in its recognition of the right to life, but in its claim that the right to life is a right that cannot be forfeited, even by a killer.

(2) *War.* As war is traditionally understood, it threatens life but not the right to life, on the grounds that it is permissible to kill a soldier who is bearing arms against you, but not permissible to kill a soldier who surrenders. This distinction has been obscured in the twentieth century by the practice of bombing enemy cities, in the inescapable knowledge that unarmed civilians are being put to death in thousands. It is therefore difficult for any nation which goes to war in modern times to pretend that it is respecting the right to life according to the traditional rules of war. Nevertheless the modern nation which

kills civilians wholesale in bombing raids, as the British did in Dresden and the Americans did in Hiroshima, still feels it can exculpate itself from moral condemnation by a plea of necessity: namely that there was no other way of defending liberty and justice and human rights against the insane aggressors who threatened world dominion in the 1940's. This plea may be considered controversial, but the important thing is that a reasonable case can be presented in support of it.

(3) *Abortion.* The practice of abortion has traditionally been considered wrong in Christian societies, and contrary to natural law, for the obvious reason that it seems to affront the right to life. In recent years abortion has found many champions, including Christian ones: and it is worthy of note that the typical argument for abortion begins with the claim that it does *not* offend the right to life, on the grounds that the foetus which is destroyed in abortions is not a developed human being, with a mind and soul, but, in the words of one Protestant divine, a mass of jelly. Clearly this is not a question on which people, including people of the highest moral scruples, are likely to agree. We see that the whole case in defence of abortion turns on the act itself being depicted as something substantially different in character from the killing of a man.

(4) *Self-defence.* Under advanced systems of positive law, the peace is kept by officers of the state, and a private man becomes unaccustomed to the practice of defending his life with his own sword or firearms. But such systems are still far from universal, and even the U.S.A. is not one of them. Killing in self-defence— or what is pleaded as self-defence—accounts for a good many lost lives. It accounted for even more, when European explorers were opening up the continent of Africa and other dark places of the world in Victorian times. But neither the armed American citizen shooting a sinister-looking figure in crime-infested streets, nor the old Empire-builder shooting savages, thinks of himself as denying the right to life. Rightly or wrongly, he regards his deed as an act of aggressive self-defence, in a dangerous situation, when to reflect too long before acting may mean a man's own death.

Throughout this catalogue of typical cases where lives are taken in the world we know, it is worth noting that however people may die, the authors of their deaths are eager to have it known that the circumstances were exceptional, and that the general right to life was being respected, even though some particular life or lives had to be ended. And leaving aside any temptation to speak of hypocrisy, this emphasis on the special character of the case may well prompt us to admit, however unwillingly, that respect for the right to life is something that men do ordinarily, and almost universally, observe.

V

The Right to Liberty

(a) Freedom of Movement

There are some grounds for thinking of the right to freedom of movement as the first and most fundamental of man's liberties. When Epictetus, for example, speaks of his freedom, he describes it in this way: 'I go wherever I wish; I come from whence I wish.'[1] The word that Epictetus uses is ἐλευθερία (eleutheria), and the etymology of this Greek word for freedom is given by one authority as παρὰ τὸ ἐλεύθειν ὅπον ἐρᾷ or 'to go where one wills'.[2] The Greeks most commonly contrasted their freedom to being bound or tied and being for this reason unable to move.[3] Being free in this most primitive sense is the opposite to bondage. To be free is to be unimpeded in the exercise of the natural desire to move. Once again, the word 'natural' is important.

One of the things that is meant by saying that men have a natural right to freedom of movement is to assert that the desire to move is a natural, universal, and reasonable one; and hence that it is not so much a man's desire to move that needs to be justified as any attempt to frustrate the satisfaction of that desire. Undoubtedly some limitations on people's freedom of movement can be justified. No reasonable person would wish to assert that the right to free movement is an absolute one and that all men have the right to go anywhere they please. There are other rights which limit this right; indeed it would be difficult to conceive of any single right except as a part of a network of rights, each of which is governed by the exigencies of others. But what are the limitations we could accept as reasonable limitations on the right to freedom of movement?

In the first place, the right to privacy and property, of which more will be said later in this essay, means that people have not the right to move freely into my house and garden. This right is sometimes exercised collectively, as in the ancient closed cities of the Orient to which no stranger was admitted; but such places are rare nowadays, and have always been rare in the West. Most civilised, and indeed most 'primitive' societies, have almost always been open to travellers. A traveller is a man who comes and goes. One of his most important defining characteristics is that he moves on. He is not a settler. The almost universal tradition of hospitality is of hospitality to a visitor. It is a tradition which recognises the natural right to move in the most literal sense; it does *not* recognise a natural right to stop and permanently stay. In the language of the French constitution of 1791, the right of movement is the *liberté d'aller, de rester, de partir.*

All nations nowadays, and most communities of the past, have regarded the permission to settle as a privilege (as opposed to a right) and some have been more sparing than others in the bestowal of this privilege. But if it is accepted that men have a right to travel, as distinct from a right to settle, then it follows that every man must needs have a right of domicile in some place to which he can return. Even though everyone has the right to move, few men have a natural desire to be always on the move. They have a natural desire for a base or homeland. This is why the natural right to movement is connected with the natural right to what we nowadays speak of as 'nationality'.[4] In a world where all the inhabitable space is divided between states, between political societies asserting the positive right to control the movements and residence of individuals, everyone needs to have his right of domicile formally recognised by one of these states. A man can no longer, as he might in earlier times, find a home in a place beyond the frontiers, where no state claims jurisdiction. In the modern world, the natural right to a domicile entails the right to formal nationality. To be 'stateless' today is in effect to be denied the natural right to a domicile; and even though most 'stateless' persons do, in fact, enjoy as a privilege the hospitality of an alien state, they are still deprived of their right.

Millions of people travel in the world today where only thousands travelled before 1914, yet the restrictions on travellers have increased. Passports were seldom needed before the First World War, and even people with a police record, such as

Lenin and his fellow revolutionaries, had little difficulty in moving about Europe. In war times in earlier centuries civilians were allowed to travel behind the enemy lines. Moreover, for several generations the New World, and other overseas territories, were open to more adventurous voyagers. In antiquity, also, people travelled a great deal. The Greek city states were sometimes inhospitable to aliens, but the Greeks themselves were free to travel, and they did travel; indeed we are told that during the Hellenistic period 'the whole world around the Mediterranean became a melting pot as a consequence of migration and the intermingling of the many nations living there'.[5] The Romans also allowed the free movement of people, and were more tolerant of immigration than had been the Greek city states. At the time of the Empire persons of foreign extraction made up almost ninety percent of the population of Rome itself.[6] The people who could *not* move freely in the ancient world were the slaves and bondsmen, and these persons were, of course, numerous. When people spoke of freedom, or *libertas*, in Rome, they conceived of this freedom, in its most simple sense, as the opposite of slavery.[7] One of the most conspicuous features of the slave was that he was a man who could not go where he wished: the free man was a man who could. Like the word '$\dot{\epsilon}\lambda\epsilon\upsilon\theta\epsilon\rho\acute{\iota}\alpha$' in Greek, the word '*libertas*' in Latin has its origins in the idea of being unimpeded in the exercise of movement.

In the Middle Ages people did not move so much: and the condition of serfdom in which many of them lived imposed restrictions somewhat similar to those endured by the slaves in the ancient world; that is, the serfs could not leave the feudal estate to which they were attached. The townspeople, who were not serfs, could come and go as they pleased, which is one of the reasons why they could say, 'City air makes a man free.'[8] Most medieval cities imposed strict controls on immigration, on newcomers settling, but not on people leaving.

If movement is expressed as 'coming and going', we may say that while some limitation on 'coming in' (and especially on settling) may be justified on the basis of the right to property, and its derivations, there is no corresponding justification to be found for laws forbidding men's 'going out'. Yet it is just such laws which have affected increasing numbers of persons in the twentieth century. In the past, it was the particular fate of slaves, bondsmen, and serfs to be forbidden to leave their place of domicile. Today millions and millions of nominal 'citizens' suffer under this interdiction. Slavery has been abolished; but when a government ordains that its people may not leave their own country without some special exit visa issued as an act of grace, that government is, in effect, imprisoning the entire people within the boundaries of its territory. Clearly the only sound justification for the imprisonment of anyone is that the person concerned has committed a crime; but the millions of people who are confined within their frontiers today are certainly not guilty, nor are they even accused of any crime.

But perhaps we shall be told, these people are not imprisoned, they are simply being 'detained' in their homeland, and detained for a legitimate purpose. What purpose could this be? It might perhaps be argued that a man may legitimately be detained in his homeland until he has discharged the national service required by the law of that state of all young adults. Such an obligation is not unreasonable, but it is a good reason for no more than a temporary limitation on movement, valid only until each person has completed his national service. If this argument is employed to sustain the assertion that the entire population is on national service from the cradle to the grave, it becomes worthless, for the expression 'national service' must then be robbed of any significance as a distinctive concept. Hence, the justification for limiting the movement out of a country of a man who has national service to complete cannot be used as a justification for limiting the movement out of the country of anybody else.

We may next ask: are there not some sound utilitarian arguments for a limitation on the right of leaving the country? It might plausibly be argued that an industrialised society needs the skill of its managerial classes or *cadres*. If substantial numbers of this class emigrate and form a 'brain drain', then the country as a whole may suffer economically. Can such people not be compelled as a whole (however unwillingly) for the sake of the others? It may well be the case that the government of the nation concerned has financed from public funds the special education and training of this *élite*; and, on the strength of this, it might be claimed that the individuals concerned have incurred a duty to stay and serve the community which has educated them. But this argument at its very best is only another form of the 'national service' argument which I have already mentioned. It justifies the keeping of a man within the boundaries of the nation only so far as is necessary for him to discharge his duties; it does not justify his being forbidden to travel during his free time for recreation or for any other reason. Still less does this argument authorise the detention of any person who has not incurred the obligation stated.

But suppose we are offered a utilitarian argument of a cruder kind: suppose someone says, 'The greatest happiness of the greater number is the only test of right and wrong, and the happiness of the whole population is better served if those individuals who want to leave the country are forbidden to leave the country.' What is being said here is that the happiness of all can be promoted by the denial of some people's reasonable claims. But what evidence is there for this belief? The happiness of a man, even by utilitarian standards, depends on the satisfaction of certain natural needs and wants. If the desire not to be in bondage is a natural desire, then men who are kept in bondage will not be happy. So you cannot make men happy by putting them in bondage and robbing them of freedom. Admittedly it is arguable in a fanciful way that you might make future generations happy by putting bonds on the present generation and forcing it to build an environment which would be more congenial than the existing environment. But this is to re-state, with a different time-dimension, one of the worst arguments that have ever been advanced in defence of slavery, namely that the misery of the enslaved persons is acceptable because it contributes to the satisfaction of the enfranchised persons. This is certainly not an argument that any serious utilitarian moral philosopher could accept, because the utilitarian appeals to the happiness of all, and not to the happiness of a section of the people: and as Bentham himself once said, the fact that pain is always more intense than pleasure means that the pleasure of some can never properly be purchased at the expense of causing pain to others. There can be no sound utilitarian argument for inflicting on men the pain of bondage, or for denying their freedom of movement in a way which is felt as a form of bondage, in the hope of producing some future pleasure for other men.

Certain types of economic theory have sometimes been invoked to justify limitations on people's freedom of movement. In the Middle Ages, the prevailing economic theories led cities to restrict immigration by prompting fears that new settlers might jeopardise the jobs and advantages of the existing inhabitants. Such restrictions, of course, applied to settlers, not visitors: and they did not affect the freedom of the inhabitants to leave their city. However, in the early modern period, the economists of mercantilism proposed new restrictions on emigration. These economists favoured *immigration*, because they believed that the larger the working population the richer the community; but, for the same reason, they opposed emigration; that is, they believed, in Sir William Petty's words, that 'fewness of people is real poverty'.[9] This economic theory prompted a reversal of medieval practice: laws against immigration were relaxed, and laws prohibiting emigration were introduced, introduced, that is, in England and France among other kingdoms. Plainly a law forbidding emigration is a far greater restriction on men's freedom of movement than is a law restricting immigration. For it is not a case of diminishing the opportunities of a foreign person who may wish to settle; it completely takes away the positive right to travel from numerous persons who were formerly free to leave.

However, the laws forbidding emigration which were enacted in France and England and elsewhere in the early modern period were not effectively enforced; and they were repealed when the economic theory of mercantilism was repudiated. This theory was falsified by events. The English workers who emigrated to the New World were found to have contributed to English prosperity. And the economists of the classical school—Adam Smith and his contemporaries—maintained that any restrictions, whether on immigration or on emigration, were injurious to the economy, and that the free movement of peoples, both in and out of the country, was in the interest of the wealth of nations.

Various communist economists of the twentieth century have revived the mercantilist argument against freedom of movement, and asserted that the policy of 'socialism in one nation' requires the confinement of the working population within its frontiers. However, in communist countries, restrictions on movement are prompted by further considerations, often by those derived from ideology. In one of its familiar formulations, communist ideology maintains that the socialist nations of the world are engaged in some form of class war, or revolutionary war, or cold war, with the capitalist powers of the world; and, hence, that communist states, being organised for their own defence on a quasi-military footing, are compelled to abridge those rights of the individual which communist ideology would be the first to respect in time of genuine peace. One objection to this way of reasoning is that it takes an argument for exceptional or emergency powers—an argument which every state employs in time of war—and applies that reasoning to the conduct of policy in ordinary times, year in, year out, in conditions which common sense would call a time of peace. The Soviet Union, from this ideological perspective, has been on a 'war footing' since it was established over fifty years ago, and some other Communist republics have been on a 'war footing' for over twenty-five years. Now a régime which claims to know no peace for such prolonged periods of time must either be reckoned to have proved a failure as a form of government, or to have developed a conception of peace so exalted as to be virtually impossible for mortal men to experience. This is one of the melancholy consequences of the whole ideological approach to politics: freedom, for the ideological mind, is possible only in a utopia, so that it is futile to expect to be able to protect and preserve the rights of man in the world of the here and now.

Various statements about human rights—even some of the United Nations' own literature commenting on the Universal Declaration—describes the rights of man as 'ideals'. This is an unfortunate word. An ideal is something which belongs to the realm of imagination and aspiration. It is something one yearns for, but cannot sensibly expect immediately to realise. But a right is not like this. It is something which *can* and should be recognised in the here and now. What ought to be done is not an ideal; what is right, what is a duty, what is just is not what it would be wise to see done one day in a better future: it is something that must be done in the present, it is something demanded by what Kant called the categorical imperative: and there can be no excuse for *not* doing it. To say that men have the right to freedom of movement is to say that those authorities who violate or thwart that right are morally at fault, and that no easy excuse can be accepted for the wrong they do.

(b) Freedom of Speech

What is meant by the assertion that men have the right to freedom of speech, that is, to freedom of utterance in both the spoken and the written form? This is often thought to mean the absence of any kind of censorship, censorship being understood as that which stands opposed to the liberty of expression. But this may be an over-simple view. Undoubtedly the very word 'censorship' has a disagreeable sound for modern ears, and rightly so; it makes us think of newspapers with blank spaces in them, of private letters being opened and read by the military, and of boards of officials scrutinising books and films to ensure that they are fit for the rest of us to see. There is something in all such arrangements which offends the sense of human dignity.

It is arguable—indeed it has been argued by Professor B. F. Skinner in his celebrated book *Beyond Freedom and Dignity*—that our conception of human dignity stands in the way of effective social engineering; but given the value that most of us still attach to the special nature of adult men and women as rational, responsible beings, the thought of being restrained and forbidden things 'for our own good' is repellent to us. Even so, it cannot be denied that censorship, in one form or another, plays a large part in all human life. The upbringing of a child, and education generally, is a prolonged exercise in censorship. In the years of our infancy, parents and teachers enact the rôle of censor; they alternately forbid things and command things; they lay down rules. Then, as a child grows up he begins to impose rules on himself. He takes the censor, so to speak, into himself. He masters his own impulses, and disciplines himself. He acquires scruples or principles, a moral sense or conscience. And as soon as he has developed his own internal censor, he ceases to need that form of censorship which has hitherto been exercised by his elders.

Much is said about the censorship of art, but art itself is more often than not the product of self-censorship. The poet writes two lines and strikes out one, or more probably, he writes thirty lines and strikes out twenty-nine. The poet who published every word he ever wrote would not be a good poet. Many artists need in their early years an external censor, in the form of a master or critic, to help them to acquire the discipline of self-censorship; Maupassant needed Flaubert, for instance, and T. S. Eliot needed Ezra Pound to act as such an external censor until each had learned to enact the rôle of censor for himself.

Important as this inner censor is, it is not the only censor that figures in adult experience. Society itself is full of different forms and forces of censorship. Codes of good behaviour and good manners imply the censorship of speech and movement in the interest of social harmony and ease. These codes are not, of course, the same in all societies, but every society has one, and even those which pride themselves on being comparatively relaxed or free still require the individual to obey fairly elaborate sets of rules and unwritten laws. The private individual must 'behave'; that is to say, he must do what is done in the milieu to which he belongs, whether it is the society of the Scottish grouse moors or that of Californian hippies. Every society, including the most 'liberated', has its unwritten law. If a man disobeys the unwritten law of good conduct under which his circumstances place him, he will be punished in all sorts of different ways: he may be reproached, he may lose friends, he may lose business or prospects of promotion; he may only incur a disapproving glance or he may be banished altogether from the company he cherishes.

In Victorian England, the middle classes lived under un-written laws of remarkable severity. John Stuart Mill's famous essay *On Liberty*, published in 1859, was directed against the oppression of these laws and not against the positive laws enforced by the British state, which were, at that time, minimal. In a memorable passage of this essay, Mill wrote that when 'society is itself the tyrant', as he put it, 'it practises a social tyranny more formidable than many kinds of political oppression, since, though not usually upheld by such extreme penalties, it leaves fewer means of escape, penetrating much more deeply into the details of life, and enslaving the soul itself. Protection, therefore, against the tyranny of the magistrate is not enough: there needs to be protection also against the tyranny of the prevailing opinion and feeling, against the tendency of society to impose by other means than civil penalties, its own ideas and practices as rules of conduct on those who dissent from them . . .'[10]

In the century and more that has passed since Mill wrote these words, the state in England has become a greater threat to liberty, while society, especially since the Second World War, has become less exigent. But a 'permissive' culture has its rules like any other: many things are still forbidden, and many things are demanded; censorship, in one form or another, is still present. If man is to live in society he must have rules; and if he does not have good ones he will have bad ones.

Censorship is a practice of all civilisations, a feature indeed of civilisation as such. For what is culture but the imposition of human design on brute nature? There are some theorists in the anarchist tradition who believe that a culture could flow from the spontaneous expression of each private person's uninhibited and unrestrained will, but there is little evidence in history or experience to justify this happy expectation. In the known world, censorship pervades and permeates all cultures. Indeed it is for this very reason that the setting up of specific governmental institutions of censorship is unnecessary. If censorship is already there, in the social fabric itself, in the whole network of relationships between men, why should there be an additional entity to make rules and give rulings?

It is because the word 'censor' has become associated in our minds with just this kind of extra or additional institution that we dislike so much the idea of censorship. It is a justified dislike. For there is a manifest affront to any society in the suggestion that its self-censorship is inadequate, and that a further political institution is needed to perform the duty. At best such a censor must be seen as a governor or guardian, whose very existence implies that the members of the society concerned are regarded as children who have not yet reached years of discretion. The existence of a state censor can only be seen as a badge of immaturity—that is, if it is not seen as a mark of servitude.

At the time when the Soviet writers Sinaievsky and Daniel were imprisoned in the U.S.S.R., and the works of Pasternak and Solzhenitsyn suppressed, it was argued by some Soviet intellectuals that the situation of literary freedom in Russia was no different from what it was in any other country. One Soviet writer, Boris Polevoi, remarked in conversation at the time: 'There is censorship everywhere.' This is a specious argument. From the premise that censorship of one kind or another is to be found in every culture, it does not follow that the kind of institutionalised censorship and dragooning of writers which prevails in the Soviet Union is to be found under all régimes. It is doubtless the case that every country has some means of limiting freedom of expression by means of laws against libel, sedition, obscenity, and blasphemy. But there is a difference between the existence of such laws and the existence of a government office to examine every manuscript before it is published. Such an institutionalised censor will give his *imprimatur* only to what the government desires the people to read. And this clearly belongs to a different category from the censorship which is exercised in the form of laws penalising those who publish utterances which can reasonably be considered injurious to people's rights.

The difference between the two kinds of censorship can be discerned in the effects. The traveller in any totalitarian country must be struck by the void on newspaper stands. Where, he may ask, are the opposition journals, the non-conforming or dissenting publications? The answer is that such journals do not exist. They have not been banned by the courts: they have never been allowed to come into existence. For this is how the institutional censor operates. Nothing can be printed or imported without his consent. He does not only suppress things, he forestalls them; like a Victorian nanny, he knows in advance what is bad for the children, and he will not admit to the nursery anything that has not been carefully vetted. A political censor who functions like this could never have a place in a free country, for the people burdened with such an institution cannot possibly acquire enough knowledge from which to form any judgement, or so to exercise freedom. Even in the Soviet Union itself the situation is felt to be intolerable, as witness the emergence in recent years of a clandestine press, written and read, at considerable risk, by people whose yearning for truth and liberty cannot be extinguished.[11]

This is not to suggest that there is no problem of censorship in a free society. Indeed, it is one characteristic feature of a free society that the workings of censorship are a continual problem to it, and a problem that is openly discussed. Different countries, and the same country at different times, will have different prevailing views as to what is, and what is not, a suitable subject for censorship. John Stuart Mill was prompted to publish his essay *On Liberty* when he discovered workmen in the public art galleries of Naples carving fig leaves for statues which had been standing naked for two thousand years. Mill wanted to restore the liberty which men had enjoyed before the rise of Puritanism. He did not advocate an absolute liberty. In some of his writings, Mill pleads for freedom only as a means to 'self-perfection'; and even in the essay *On Liberty* he says that liberty should not be extended to actions which affect others besides the man who acts.

It must, however, be said that Mill's argument on this question is not a satisfactory one. Mill tried to divide the things men do and say into two distinct categories, into what he called 'self-regarding actions' and 'other-regarding actions'. Mill suggested that actions of the first kind should be tolerated, and those of the second kind not. He claimed that actions such as the observation of the Sabbath were a man's own business. A man should be allowed to decide for himself whether to go to Church or work in his garden on a Sunday, because only the man himself was affected by what he did. It was of no concern to other people; and therefore other people had no right, Mill said, to demand that a man leave his garden and go to Church. The weakness of Mill's argument is that he fails to see that practically everything anyone does is of some concern to others beside the agent. If I am a Churchgoer, I care very much whether my neighbours are with me or not; worship is a social exercise, so my neighbour's decision to stay in his garden is not simply a 'self-regarding action'. Mill even suggests that whether a man gets drunk or not is of no one's concern but his own. In fact, of course, excessive drinking nearly always affects other people beside the drinker, especially those who care for, or are dependent on, him. Mill's whole class of 'self-regarding actions' turns out to be very small indeed.

What Mill had in mind when he invented the phrase 'other-regarding actions' was the kind of action which harms or injures people other than the agent. This is in keeping with his general utilitarian belief that evil is what causes some kind of pain. But here again it is hard to discover a clear-cut explanation of what harm is, and still more difficult to find common agreement as to what constitutes potential harm. Mill would say, and perhaps any utilitarian would have to say, that the only justification of censorship was the prevention of harm. And those of us who are not utilitarians, those who would prefer perhaps to say that the justification of censorship was its necessary share in the conservation of values, might readily agree with Mill that the prevention of harm would be a sound justification, if not the only justification, of censorship.

Now it may well be asked: What pain can be caused by words? How can freedom of expression injure anyone? Broadly speaking there appear to be four kinds of utterance which have been commonly considered harmful: the libellous, the obscene, the blasphemous and the seditious. It is worth considering each of these in turn.

A libel or slander is a form of utterance which injures an individual in his honour, dignity, or reputation. Here the element of injury is present, so to speak, in the definition of the term: what remains to be determined is the extent of the injury done in any particular instance. So matters of libel are generally left to the arbitration of law courts.

Obscenity has been prosecuted by positive law in all societies, and some societies—such as that of Victorian England against which Mill reacted—had very few doubts about what obscenity meant. But more recently Western societies, at any rate, have ceased to have any generally agreed views as to what is or is not obscene. Indeed, so far as English law is concerned, the highest courts have stated that the legal definition of 'obscenity' is not the same as the everyday definition of 'obscenity', the former having to do mainly with corruption and the latter with indecency. But however the word 'obscenity' is interpreted, a reasonable case can be made for limiting the freedom of speech in the interests both of public decency and of protecting vulnerable persons from the kind of utterance which stirs up base and ignoble passions. Even in Denmark, where most known forms of pornography are tolerated, there remain restrictions on other kinds of obscenity; to put the point more fairly, in Denmark, where pornography is tolerated, it is tolerated because it is no longer considered obscene, and what is still thought obscene is not tolerated. The difficulty is to delineate the category clearly. Perhaps there have never been any hard edges around it, and in Western societies the edges are today more blurred than ever. Nevertheless there are extremes of obscenity which the most 'permissive' society could not tolerate. It is difficult to give an example of what this might be. But some standards of public decency are necessary to any civilisation: and every society must defend the basic values which give it cohesion.

The third category of speech or writing which is subject to censorship is the blasphemous. This may well sound like an out-of-date category. In France, in Voltaire's time, a young noble-man was executed by a cruel method for singing a blasphemous song in the street. Even in England in Mill's time, a man was sent to jail for writing an irreverent reference to Christ on a village wall. Such things no longer happen. Remarks that past generations would have considered outrageously blasphemous are freely uttered on modern television programmes, and effectively pass unnoticed.

But it would be a mistake to conclude that blasphemy no longer troubles people. A new kind of secular blasphemy has arisen with the secular ideologies of the twentieth century. One of the reasons given for the suppression of Pasternak's novel *Dr Zhivago* was that the author wrote disrespectfully of the achievements of the Bolshevik Revolution. There have been cases in Greece of writers being imprisoned for speaking dis-respectfully of the military régime. The offence in such cases is that of writing in an impudent or insolent fashion about that which is thought to be sacred and to require veneration. The offence may not be called 'blasphemy', but that is what it comes down to; and the more secular institutions are allowed to claim divinity, the more widespread this offence is likely to become in the future. Blasphemy has nearly always been severely punished, and we must clearly await the emergence of a more sceptical age than our own before blasphemy ceases to be reckoned a crime.

The fourth class of utterance which is commonly denied freedom is the seditious. Sedition is an attempt to undermine the constitution and imperil the safety of the state. In theory there is no doubt about the harmfulness of it. But there is an ambiguity in all the words invoked to explain it. In Mr Smith's Rhodesia, for example, a government which is itself considered by many jurists to be unlawful has accused and even imprisoned some of its opponents for the crime of sedition. In England in the seventeenth century, King Charles I and King James II accused their enemies of sedition, and were themselves accused in turn of having acted seditiously against the constitution.

And what of sedition in a country where the régime has suppressed the opposition altogether? In such places it is impossible to change the government without a revolution. Indeed one of the greatest criticisms that can be addressed to a totalitarian, or even to a one-party, system is that such systems transform opposition to the government into sedition against the state. Since it would be folly to suggest that all opposition to governments is harmful, we cannot say that everything which is condemned as seditious is necessarily wrong.

So again we reach a paradoxical conclusion: it is reasonable that freedom of expression should stop short at the seditious, but there can be no clear general rule for determining in actual cases what should, and should not, be counted as sedition. This is consequently a matter of practical wisdom. Where things cannot be known, they must be settled by discussion.

VI

The Right to Property

There is something absurd about asking: 'Is there a right to property?' for the simple reason that the word 'property' by definition implies a right. 'Property' means 'rightful ownership'; and the difference between possession and property is that the latter adds to the mere fact of having and holding the title to have and to hold. The word 'property' both names and claims. Proudhon's famous remark 'Property is theft' is, on the face of it, a contradiction in terms, since the one word means lawful holding and the other unlawful seizing. I say 'on the face of it' because Proudhon's paradox was intended to be understood as saying something meaningful; he was asserting that the system of positive law in nineteenth-century France recognised as 'property' possessions which the bourgeoisie had gained, he believed, by robbing the working classes of the fruits of their labour. Proudhon claimed that the workers had the *natural* right to ownership; and it was because the bourgeoisie enjoyed the *positive* right, that he assailed the existing institutions of property as being, from his point of view, unlawful; not contrary to positive law, of course, but contrary to natural law.

To assert, as do so many statements of the rights of man, that man has a right to property, is not to assert that everyone has the right in natural law to whatever possessions he is allowed to enjoy by the system of positive law under which he lives. The numerous cases of exiled criminals in South America having their ill-gotten fortunes recognised as legitimate possessions should make us aware of the ambiguity of the word 'property' —an ambiguity which corresponds to that of the word 'rights' with which it is logically connected. Possession may be rightful in positive law, but not rightful in natural or moral law; although either form of rightfulness will justify the use of the word 'property' in speaking of such possession.

Of all political philosophers, it was Locke who had the most to say about the natural right to property, and he was indeed rather proud of the argument he had developed to vindicate the existence of such a natural right.[1] Locke's method was, very simply, to employ the most usual and effective plea for the justification of any right; he argued in effect that the right concerned was one that had been earned. Locke traced the origin of property to a man's natural duty to work for the provision of his own food and shelter, and he suggested that a man gained the right to ownership of that part of nature with which he mixed his labour. The acorns that a man gathered, or the game that he hunted, were his because he had worked to possess them. Locke does not fail to observe that property relationships become more complex with the introduction of money, and he goes on to suggest that the right to property extends to possessions which are not the fruits of a man's own labour, precisely because men give tacit consent to the introduction of money. In more advanced societies, wealth, and especially large estates, are normally acquired by inheritance, or received in the form of rent and interest, none of which is the product of the owner's work. Locke gives good grounds for thinking that the existence of private fortunes, based on inheritance, rent or interest, are of general social utility, in promoting economic growth and so forth, and hence that such property rights are valid; but these arguments are somewhat removed from the natural law argument which Locke gives for right of property in the fruits of a man's own labour. So Locke could be cited by Marx as readily as he was cited by Adam Smith.

The institution of property derives in part from the human condition. Scarcity prevails in nature. Man is not only vulnerable in the sense that he is very easily killed or injured. He is also bound by his own needs to work for a living. Food does not grow abundantly on every tree. Natural caves do not provide adequate shelter for every human being. Food can be found by the seeker, or grown by the planter; but neither exercise is easy; and even the foodstuffs produced by these efforts perish rapidly; so there is no end to the travail of struggling to survive. What is hard-earned a man will naturally and fairly feel entitled to keep: as keep he must if he is to survive through the winters of his life, when nature is not merely niggardly, but cruelly and almost totally unyielding. At this level, the right to property can be derived from the right to life: if a man is entitled to survive, he is entitled to retain the possessions necessary to his survival. Some philosophers, including St Thomas Aquinas, have suggested that the right to life, being prior to the right to property, allows a starving man to steal to keep himself alive; or, more exactly, that it is not stealing (i.e., culpable dispossession) for a starving man to take from another a loaf of bread. Locke disagreed: he said that the richer man had the duty to give the bread to the starving man; but that the starving man had no right to take it. The difference, perhaps, reflects a difference between the medieval and the modern Christian *ethos*. Attitudes to property are bound to differ from one culture to another, and no expression of a universal right to property can be other than exceedingly abstract.

It might well be said that everyone has the right to whatever property he has honestly and lawfully acquired, except that which is lawfully demanded of him as taxation by the system of government under which he lives. We have already noted the ambiguity of the word 'lawfully'; what is more, the qualification concerning taxation lends itself to limitless exploitation. A left-wing régime which strips a man of almost all his goods may plead that it is doing no more than imposing taxation. It is commonly said that taxation is legitimate only when it is voluntary: but just how 'voluntary' are the enormous taxes which are paid in some twentieth-century welfare states, for example, taxes often paid grudgingly by men whose only motive for paying is to avoid the penalties attached to non-payment? At what point does high taxation become confiscation? Has President Allende in Chile already crossed the line, as Dr Castro in Cuba crossed it years ago? In speaking of taxation, we are moving in another area where all the edges are blurred, although we can point to extreme cases, at the one extreme, of taxes willingly paid, and at the other, of undisguised confiscation.

The significance of confiscation is not simply that it deprives men of their property, but that it deprives them of their liberty as well. It may well be that man's natural right to property can, if taken in isolation, be justified only to the extent that the right is an earned right; but it must not be forgotten that the right to property is one member of a family of rights, intimately related to the right to freedom; and it is hard to conceive how men can possibly be free if they have no right to possessions, and are wholly dependent for the necessities and comforts of their lives on the grace of some lord or master or communistic government. Property in this sense is inseparable from liberty.

VII

The Protection of Human Rights

One of the difficulties which confront the student of human rights in the world today is that of ascertaining how far the nominal 'legal rights' specified in the written laws of different states are in fact positive rights. On paper, the position is most satisfactory. In capitalist and socialist countries alike, and in the new republics of the Third World, constitutions affirm, or even 'guarantee', the historic rights of man as the rights of the inhabitants. But when we pass from the examination of written laws and constitutions to that of the actual practice of governments, the story is a very different one. The historic rights of man are positive rights in only a limited number of countries. The missing factor is enforcement. And how is that to be provided? If particular governments choose not to enforce the rights which they are obliged by their own constitutions to uphold, what is there to be done about it? If a man is deprived of his rights by his rulers, to whom can he appeal?

The late Judge Lauterpächt, in a book[1] he wrote just after the last war, argued that the protection of human rights depended largely on the institution of a new international body with this specific purpose. Lauterpächt himself was a judge of the International Court of Justice at The Hague; but this is a court to which states alone have access. He wished to see a court set up to which individuals could apply for redress, if their own government failed to respect their rights. As it was, it appeared to Lauterpächt, writing in 1950, that the people whose rights were best protected were those who lived in the Trust Territories of the United Nations, because they had the opportunity to appeal, beyond their own government to the Trusteeship Council of the United Nations if they believed that their rights had been violated. Judge Lauterpächt looked forward to the creation of similar United Nations institutions for the protection of everyone's rights. In the twenty years and more that have passed since he wrote the Trust Territories have virtually disappeared with the creation of new sovereign states, but new United Nations institutions have failed to materialise. Yet the United Nations has continued to talk about human rights almost continuously, passing resolutions, holding meetings of special councils and commissions, initiating covenants, conventions and treaties, and publishing documents. It has certainly not lost interest in the subject.

The obligations of the U.N. in the matter of human rights are well known. Article 55 of its Charter stipulates that the United Nations shall promote 'respect for, and observance of, human rights and fundamental freedoms'; and Article 56 requires that 'all members pledge themselves to take joint and separate action in co-operation . . . for the achievement of the purposes set forth in Article 55'. Two questions immediately arise: What are these 'human rights and fundamental freedoms'? And what has the United Nations done 'to promote respect for and observation of them'? The 'Nuclear' Commission on Human Rights appointed by the Economic and Social Council of the United Nations held its inaugural meeting in May 1946, when the first of its allotted tasks was to submit to the General Assembly recommendations and reports regarding 'An International Bill of Rights'. Mrs Eleanor Roosevelt, of the United States, was elected chairman of the 'full' Commission on Human Rights, and the other countries represented were Nationalist China, France, Lebanon, Australia, Belgium, Byelorussia, Chile, Egypt, India, Iran, Panama, the Philippine Republic, the U.S.S.R., the United Kingdom, Uruguay, and Yugoslavia. The United Kingdom at once put forward a draft Bill of Rights in the form of a convention or treaty which both named the specific human rights to be recognised and provided for international machinery to deal with alleged violations of these rights. The British delegation not unnaturally interpreted the expression 'Bill of Rights' as meaning an instrument of positive law, and therefore understood the duty of the Commission to be that of finding a formula for making human rights enforceable, and thus transforming them into positive rights. In this the British were supported by the Indians, and also by the Australian representative, who put forward detailed proposals for setting up an International Court of Human Rights which would sit in judgement in the case of any alleged violations of the rights as specified in the proposed Bill. The Soviet representative criticised these proposals. He protested that it was 'premature' to discuss any measure of a binding or judicial nature. The U.S.S.R. was willing to support a Bill of Rights, but only a 'Bill' understood as a manifesto of rights. Failing to agree on what a 'Bill' meant, the commission settled on a compromise. If it could not produce one document it would produce two. First there would be a manifesto or declaration 'defining in succinct terms the fundamental rights and freedoms of man which, according to Article 55 of the Charter, the United Nations must promote'. Later there would be 'something more legally binding than a mere Declaration', and this second instrument it was decided to call a Covenant.

The full text of the Universal Declaration of Human Rights is considerably longer than the declarations issued in the Age of Reason, though not necessarily better. In the early articles of the Universal Declaration the language is that of the old natural rights tradition. The rights to life, liberty, property, equality, justice, and the pursuit of happiness are spelled out in twenty articles, which name, among other things, the right to freedom of movement, the right to own property alone as well as in association with others, the right to marry, the right to equality before the law and to a fair trial if accused of any crime, the right to privacy, the right to religious freedom, the right to free speech and peaceful assembly, the right to asylum. Among the practices outlawed are slavery, torture, and arbitrary detention. The Universal Declaration of 1948 does not, however, limit itself to this elaboration of the classical principles. It includes a further set of articles which name rights of another kind. Article 20 asserts that everyone 'has the right to social security', and further articles proclaim the universal right to education, the right to equal pay for equal work, the right of everyone to 'a standard of living . . . adequate for the health and well-being of himself and his family', and, what is even more novel, the right to rest, leisure, and 'periodic holidays with pay'.

The difference between these new rights and the traditional natural rights was not unnoticed by those responsible for drafting the Declaration. In the records of the commission, the rights named in the first twenty articles are called 'political and civil rights' and the new rights are called 'economic and social rights'. I shall now adopt this terminology. The inclusion of economic and social rights in the Universal Declaration represented a considerable diplomatic gain for the Communist members of the United Nations, even though, when it came to the point, the Soviet Union did not vote for the Universal Declaration of 1948, but abstained: so that the Declaration was 'passed and proclaimed' *nemine contradicente* rather than unanimously.

Economic and social rights were unknown to Locke and the other natural rights theorists of the past, and it may be thought a mark of progress that they should be considered human rights today. But there is a danger here of men's hearts prevailing over their heads; and I shall argue in a later chapter that 'economic and social rights' cannot logically be considered universal human rights, and that the attempt to do so has vitiated the whole enterprise of protecting human rights through the United Nations. Many people, of course, besides Communists believe in the concept of economic and social rights; but the diplomatic advantage which Communist governments acquired from the inclusion of such rights in the Universal Declaration is that it enabled them to claim, truthfully, that a substantial proportion of the rights proclaimed were already upheld by their régimes. Assuredly, the Communist governments could not seriously claim that they upheld the rights to liberty, property, or security from arbitrary arrest, secret trials or forced labour: but they could fairly claim to provide universal education, social security, and 'periodic holidays with pay'.

However, the Universal Declaration of 1948 was not presented to the world, even by those who framed it, as something to be taken *au pied de la lettre*. It was put forward as a provisional document, a statement of ideals: 'Now therefore the General Assembly proclaims this Universal Declaration of Human Rights as a common standard of achievement for all peoples and all nations . . .' But even the General Assembly was not satisfied with this pious utterance. The Commission on Human Rights was instructed in 1948 'as a matter of priority' to complete the task of producing something that would be legally binding, namely 'a draft convention on human rights and draft measures of implementation'.[2]

This 'covenant' soon became two covenants, because the Commission having once become aware of a difference in kind between the traditional rights of man and new 'economic and social' rights, soon realised that they could not be implemented by the same procedures. In both cases the rights had to be re-stated once again; and framed, moreover, in language which would impose an intelligible commitment on the member states of the United Nations. It was the covenant, after all, which was to transform nominal rights into positive rights. The proceedings at the United Nations soon began to slow down. And as the years passed, some members of the United Nations Commission on Human Rights—not only Communists—began to mistrust the whole enterprise. They started to protest that the setting up of any international machinery for the implementation of human rights 'would tend to undermine the sovereignty and independence of States'.

By 1950 the majority of the Commission was still in favour of some system of implementation. There were various proposals regarding the establishment of an international court of human rights, of *ad hoc* committees or permanent organs, which would settle disputes arising out of the interpretation or application of the covenant or otherwise supervise the observance of its provisions, and to which either states alone or individuals and groups as well as states, might submit petitions or applications. There was an even division of opinion as to whether states only should have access to the proposed court, or whether petitions from individuals and non-governmental organisations should also be received. This was noted at the Fifth Session of the Commission on Human Rights. At its Sixth Session (March–May 1950) the even division of opinion had hardened into a majority against petitions from individuals or non-governmental organisations being received. The Commission decided to recommend the setting up of a permanent juridical body, to be called the Human Rights Committee, which 'would receive any complaint by any State Party to the covenant that another State Party was not giving effect to any provision thereof'.

However, at the Fifth Session of the General Assembly, held in September–December of the same year, a resolution was passed instructing the Commission on Human Rights 'to proceed with the consideration of provisions to be inserted in the draft covenant or separate protocols for the receipt and examination of petitions from *individuals and organisations*'.[3] At its next meeting, the Commission on Human Rights reaffirmed its proposal that the 'measures of implementation to be included in the first draft covenant' (i.e., the one concerning political rights) 'should include provisions for consideration of state-to-state complaints'; and at the same meeting, it rejected again, in face of the General Assembly's resolution, the proposal to give the right to individuals by eight votes to three, with three abstentions; and the proposal to give the right to non-governmental organisations was rejected by seven votes to four with three abstentions.[4]

The English-speaking delegations, which in the early days of the Commission had been so eager to establish a court to make human rights positive rights, were now on the side of circumspection.[5] The United Nations secretariat sent out a questionnaire on the right of petition to member States, and the replies make instructive reading. Israel and the Philippines were in favour of non-governmental organisations as well as states having the right of petition, but opposed the right being extended to individuals; Denmark proposed dealing with the problem by separate agreements; Holland and Australia thought that 'for the present' only states should be admitted to the right of petition. India put forward the proposal that an Attorney-General or High Commissioner should be appointed to present cases to the court or committee on behalf of individuals or non-governmental organisations. On the other hand, the United States, the United Kingdom, Norway, France, and Yugoslavia replied in favour of the right of petition being confined to states only.

Some of the governments which answered the questionnaire

gave the reasons for their views. The United Kingdom argued that if the right of petition were extended to individuals it would be abused; it would raise too many difficulties, and 'would place in jeopardy all the work which has been devoted' to preparing the covenants. France put forward the view that as there was not universal acceptance of the right of petition being given to individuals and unofficial bodies it would be worse than useless to try to bring about its establishment by a majority decision. France would support it only if everybody else did.

These arguments, and others, can be found in the records of the Commission on Human Rights itself. The governments which resisted the right of individual petition made much of the consideration that the 'international community was not sufficiently developed', and that the right of petition would be abused by frivolous, crankish, or litigious persons suffering from persecution mania. Other arguments invoked were: (1) that only states could be subjects of international law; (2) that the right of petition being extended to individuals would be a threat to national sovereignty; (3) that there was no reason for doubting that States Parties would fulfil their obligations.[6]

Against these views, it was maintained by other members of the Commission (1) that international law is *not* only concerned with relations between states, the League of Nations' work for minorities and the Nuremberg Trials having afforded precedents of another kind; (2) that any restriction of national sovereignty arising from the covenants would be *voluntary*; (3) that there was in some cases reason for doubting that States Parties would fulfil their obligations.[7]

It was the former set of arguments which won the day. The first covenant, the one on civil and political rights, contains no fewer than fifty clauses. A large proportion, namely articles 28–45, simply set out and delimit the powers of the Committee to be set up to sit in judgement on the petitions of states. The earlier articles repeat in more elaborate and at the same time more guarded language the political rights—or at any rate *some* of the political rights named in the Universal Declaration. Article 2 obliges every contracting state to 'adopt such legislation and other measures as may be necessary to give effect to the rights recognised in the present covenant'. Article 3 affirms the equality between men and women; article 4 allows the States Parties to the covenant 'in time of public emergency which threatens the life of the nation' to take some measures 'derogating from their obligations under the present covenant to the extent strictly required by the exigencies of the situation'.

One clause specifies that 'no one shall be arbitrarily deprived of his life' (article 6); others prohibit torture and 'cruel, inhuman or degrading treatment or punishment' (article 7); and forbid slavery, the slave trade and forced labour, but specifically permit compulsory military and other national service (article 8). Article 9 asserts that 'everyone has the right to liberty and security of person', and that 'no one shall be deprived of his liberty except on such grounds, and in accordance with such procedures as are established by law'; article 10 calls for the humane treatment of persons detained; article 11 says that there shall be no imprisonment for inability to fulfil contract; article 12 lays down the right of everyone to move freely within his own country and to leave any country including his own, a right subject only to restrictions 'which are provided by law and necessary to protect national security, public order, health or morals, or the rights and freedoms of others, and are consistent with the other rights recognised in the present covenant'. Article 13 forbids any expulsion of aliens except that which is 'lawful'; article 14 affirms the right to a fair trial for accused persons; article 15 prohibits retroactive punishments; article 16 demands the recognition of everyone as a person before the law; article 17 affirms the right to privacy and protection of family, home, correspondence, honour and reputation. Article 19 asserts the right to freedom of expression, while articles 21 and 22 specify in turn the right to assembly and association.

The remaining clauses name the right to free association, including the right to form and join trade unions (article 22); the right of men and women of marriageable age to marry (article 23); the right of every child, whatever its race, to a name and to protection as a minor (article 24): the right of every citizen to vote (article 25); the right to equality before the law (article 26) and the right of ethnic minorities to their own culture (article 27).

A significant article of the Covenant provides for the setting up of a Human Rights Committee authorised 'to receive and consider communications to the effect that a State party claims that another State party is not fulfilling its obligations under the present Covenant' (article 41). Access to the Committee is, as we have noted, expressly limited to States.

The Covenant on Civil and Political Rights, together with the further Covenant on Economic and Social Rights, was approved by the General Assembly of the United Nations in December 1966, by a substantial majority. But approval did not go much further. A minimum of 35 ratifications of the Covenant was needed to bring them into operation, and even after several years those ratifications were not forthcoming.[8] Still more unacceptable to member States was the optional Protocol granting individual access to the United Nations Committee on Human Rights. Only a handful of governments has ratified that. One proposal which seemed likely to be salvaged to provide some small measure of concrete protection for human rights through the United Nations was the Indian idea, revived in 1965 by Costa Rica, for appointing a High Commissioner for Human Rights. In 1967, the Economic and Social Council[9] approved a draft resolution to establish such an office 'with the degree of independence and prestige required'. Even this High Commissioner was to be restricted, however, to promoting human rights 'at the request of a member State'. The proposal to appoint a High Commissioner was on the agenda of the General Assembly by 1970, but it was deferred, with several amendments, until the 28th session of the General Assembly in 1973.

In the meantime a great deal had been said in the various organs of the United Nations about human rights, and especially about the economic and social rights. But nothing remotely resembling action took place. Indeed, on the matter of implementation, the covenant on economic and social rights offers nothing. It does not even propose an institution to adjudicate on disputes between states. There is only the vacuous formula of 'periodic reports'. The value of such 'reports' may be judged by any reader of the United Nations *Yearbooks on Human Rights*, where representatives of the various member states take it in turn each to boast of the deeds his government has done to uphold the rights of man: an uninspiring performance in almost every case.

A new right which did not appear in the Universal Declaration of 1948 figures in Article 1 of the United Nation Covenants: this asserts the right of all peoples to self-determination. There is something peculiar about this right. All the other rights belong to 'man' understood as individual man and woman: in the language of the Universal Declaration they are rights that 'everyone' has. Clearly, the right of *a people* to self-determination or anything else cannot be a right in this sense. It is a collective right; the right of a group and not of a person.

But what constitutes a people? Are the inhabitants of Provence or Brittany or Wales or Cornwall or Quebec a 'people'? Each is undoubtedly an ethnic or cultural group, distinct in some ways from the other inhabitants of the political society to which it at present belongs. Do the inhabitants of these areas have a right to separate self-determination which the governments of France, Canada, and the United Kingdom, as signatories of the United Nations Covenant, ought now to concede?

There is clearly no uniformity in the way governments behave in this matter. The inhabitants of Bangladesh were acknowledged to be a people in 1971 and their right of self-determination was duly recognised elsewhere.[10] But the inhabitants of Biafra were denied the status of a people a few years earlier: and far from having their right of self-determination admitted by the United Nations, such leading member-states of the United Nations as Great Britain and Russia vied with one another in providing arms for the Federation of Nigeria to extinguish Biafra. The United States fought in the 1860's to resist the claim of the Confederation of the Southern States to independence, and fought again in 1917 to uphold the claims of various Balkan communities to independence. The United Nations itself sent forces to protect the South

Korean people's right to self-determination, and later sent forces to thwart the secession of Katanga from the Congo.

Whether a group of people constitutes 'a people' seems more often than not to depend on the fortunes of war and the strategic interests of great powers. Bangladesh acquired the right to self-determination when might was on its side. Unlike the Biafrans, who had no foreign allies, the inhabitants of Bangladesh had the support of the Indian Army in their claim to constitute 'a people', and therefore to be entitled in the eyes of the world to self-determination. 'Rights' in the sense of just entitlement seems to have played a minor role in the case. The 'rights of a people' are distinct from the rights of man, and whether they are enjoyed or not is a question that is usually settled by force.

* * *

The United Nations is not the only international body which is interested in human rights. There is also the Council of Europe at Strasbourg, which has succeeded in bringing into existence some of the instruments for the enforcement of human rights which the United Nations once contemplated and then rejected. In 1950 foreign ministers of fifteen European states signed a 'European Covenant for the protection of Human Rights and Fundamental Freedoms', and in 1952 they approved the text of a Protocol specifying three further rights. Those represented were the United Kingdom, Belgium, Denmark, France, Western Germany, Iceland, Eire, Italy, Luxembourg, Saar, Turkey, Greece, Norway, Sweden, and Holland. Austria subscribed to the Covenant when she joined the Council of Europe in 1956. From the beginning the Council of Europe set itself to move on from the enumeration of human rights to 'the universal and effective recognition' of them; and the preamble to the European Covenant expressed the resolution of the high contracting parties 'as the governments of European countries which are like-minded and have a common heritage of political traditions, ideals, freedom, and the rule of law, to take the first steps for the *collective enforcement* [my italics] of certain of the rights stated in the Universal Declaration proclaimed by the United Nations in 1948'.

The specific rights which the signatories agreed to protect were the traditional political rights, notably the rights to life, liberty, and security of person; freedom from slavery, torture, and forced labour; the right on criminal charges to a fair and public trial; the right to privacy; freedom of thought, conscience, and religion; freedom of expression and assembly; the right to form trade unions and the right to marry. Article 14 states:

> 'The enjoyment of the rights and freedoms set forth in this Covenant shall be secured without discrimination on any ground such as sex, race, colour, language, religion, political or other opinion, national or social origin, association with a national minority, property, birth or other status.'

The protocol of 1952 gave recognition to the right of property (subject to the right of a government to impose taxes and 'control the use of property as it thinks fit'); the right to education (the state 'shall respect the right of parents to ensure such education and teaching in conformity with their own religious and philosophical convictions')[11] and the right to political suffrage (the signatories 'undertake to hold free elections at reasonable intervals by secret ballot').

The importance of this European Covenant, however, lies not so much in the rights it specifies as in the fact that it contains binding commitments and that it set up new international legal institutions. The two innovations of the Council are the European Commission for Human Rights and the European Court of Human Rights. These two institutions are open to receive petitions from individuals who believe that their rights, as defined in the European Covenant, are being violated. The only proviso is that the Court shall deal only with cases which come under the jurisdiction of governments which recognise the authority of the Court. Applications from one state against another can also be entertained.

Of the two bodies, the Commission is the first to consider any petition or complaint. Its members are equal in number to that of the contracting parties. In order to prevent governments having to deal with a vast number of vexatious or unfounded petitions, the Commission has a sub-committee to weed out such cases and to conduct preliminary enquiries.

When cases are accepted as *bona fide* they are first referred to governments, and efforts are made to settle them by amicable negotiations. If these fail, the Commission has the ultimate remedy of referring the case to the European Court of Human Rights. The Commission is only partly a judicial body, having at the same time fact-finding and diplomatic duties; it also holds its meetings in private, while the European Court of Human Rights is a public court of justice in the full sense of that term. Those who sit on the Court are all professional judges; they are elected by the Consultative Assembly of the Council of Europe for a term of nine years. The Commission first acquired powers to consider petitions in July 1955; the Court met to hear its first case in October 1960, and has since heard several of considerable interest.

In the past, international courts of justice have dealt only incidentally and peripherally with human rights. The Strasbourg Court can find some precedent in the Mixed Commission for Upper Silesia set up by the Geneva Convention on Minorities in 1922, and in the Court of Central America. Even so the Strasbourg Court makes legal history by the breadth of its competence, and because the Convention not only confers, through the Commission, a right of petition by individuals against their own governments but also allows, in principle, an appeal by an individual even if not a national of a Member State of the Council of Europe. It might well be asked: What are the prospects for the enlargement and extension of the kind of institution which has been set up by the Council of Europe? One can hardly fail to remark about the Strasbourg court that it protects the human rights of the people who need it least. The inhabitants of Northern and Western Europe, whose governments allow their citizens access to the Strasbourg court are already among the freest people in the world; their human rights are already well protected by domestic or municipal law. Those who live in Greece and Turkey are less well placed, even though their countries are member States of the Council of Europe. There can be no denying that the kind of human rights which are named in the European Covenant have been openly violated by the Colonels' régime in Greece, and, on a lesser scale, by the government of

Turkey. The government of Turkey could fairly plead that the activities of terrorists made it necessary to abridge civil rights in Turkey, and since the British government was put in a similar predicament by terrorists in Northern Ireland, the Turkish government's plea found at least some sympathetic listeners. Greece, however, has proved a lasting embarrassment to the whole human rights policy of the Council of Europe, and it brings us back once more to the question of enforcement. If a supra-national court like that of Strasbourg has no force at its disposal, how can it implement a decision in favour of an individual's right, when the sovereign power of the territory where that individual finds himself decides to act as it thinks best and ignore the findings of the court? And what can the Council of Europe do if no petition to the commission and court at Strasbourg is allowed by the governments concerned? There is the sanction of expulsion (favoured by some Scandinavians): but if that sanction is not seriously feared by such a government as that of Greece, which simply ceased in 1970 to be a party to the Convention on Human Rights, the Council of Europe can be of no efficacy in relieving any injury done to an individual in Greece or elsewhere. The institutions of 'collective enforcement' provided by the European Covenant of 1950 have yet to fulfil their promise.

VIII

Economic and Social Rights

It is said that when that remarkable American jurist Wesley Newcomb Hohfeld tried to make the students at Yale Law School discriminate carefully between different uses of the term 'right' in Anglo-American law, he earned himself considerable unpopularity; his pupils even got up a petition to have him removed from his Chair.[1] If the analysis of positive rights is thus resisted by law students we should not be surprised if the analysis of human rights is ill-regarded by many politicians, publicists, and even political theorists. Some politicians, indeed, have a vested interest in keeping talk about human rights as meaningless as possible. For there are those who do not want to see human rights become positive rights by genuine enactments; hence the more nebulous, unrealistic, or absurd the concept of human rights is made out to be, the better such men are pleased.

I believe that a philosophically respectable concept of human rights has been muddled, obscured, and debilitated in recent years by an attempt to incorporate into it specific rights of a different logical category. The traditional human rights are political and civil rights such as the right to life, liberty, and a fair trial. What are now being put forward as universal human rights are economic and social rights, such as the right to unemployment insurance, old-age pensions, medical services, and holidays with pay. There is both a philosophical and a political objection to this. The philosophical objection is that the new theory of human rights does not make sense. The political objection is that the circulation of a confused notion of human rights hinders the effective protection of what are correctly seen as human rights.

* * *

At the United Nations interest in political and civil rights has tended over the years to give way to consideration of economic and social rights. The reasons for this I shall discuss in a later chapter. In 1966, the two sets of rights were accorded more or less equal status in the simultaneous reception by the General Assembly of the two Covenants, the one on political and civil, the other on economic and social rights. And while the great majority of governments has procrastinated in the matter of ratifying either Covenant, the Covenant on economic and social rights has proved the more popular. There is one good reason for this easy popularity of the second covenant: and that is that the rights it names are not universal human rights at all.

There is nothing essentially difficult about transforming political and civil rights into positive rights. All that is needed is an international court with real powers of enforcement. But the so-called economic and social rights cannot be transformed into positive rights by analogous innovations. A right is like a duty in that it must pass the test of practicability. It is not my duty to do what it is physically impossible for me to do. You cannot reasonably say that it was my duty to have jumped into the River Thames at Richmond to rescue a drowning child if I was nowhere near Richmond at the time the child was drowning. What is true of duties is equally true of rights. If it is impossible for a thing to be done, it is absurd to claim it as a right. At present it is utterly impossible, and will be for a long time yet, to provide 'holidays with pay' for everybody in the world. For millions of people who live in those parts of Asia, Africa, and South America where industrialisation has hardly begun, such claims are vain and idle.

The traditional 'political and civil rights' can (as I have said) be readily secured by legislation; and generally they can be secured by fairly simple legislation. Since those rights are for the most part rights against government interference with a man's activities, a large part of the legislation needed has to do no more than restrain the government's own executive arm. This is no longer the case when we turn to 'the right to work', 'the right to social security', and so forth. For a government to provide social security it needs to do more than make laws; it has to have access to great capital wealth, and many governments in the world today are still poor. The government of India, for example, simply cannot command the resources that would guarantee each one of over 500 million inhabitants of India 'a standard of living adequate for the health and well-being of himself and his family', let alone 'holidays with pay'.

Another test of a human right is that it shall be a genuinely universal moral right. This the so-called human right to holidays with pay plainly cannot pass. For it is a right that is necessarily limited to those persons who are *paid* in any case, that is to say, to the *employé* class. Since not everyone belongs to this class, the right cannot be a universal right, a right which, in the terminology of the Universal Declaration, 'everyone' has. That the right to a holiday with pay is for many people a real moral right, I would not for one moment deny. But it is a right which falls into section (2) (b) of the classification of rights which I have set out in Chapter 3; that is, a right which can be claimed by members of a specific class of persons *because* they are members of that class.

A further test of a human right, or universal moral right, is the test of *paramount importance*. Here the distinction is less definite, but no less crucial. And here again there is a parallel between rights and duties. It is a paramount duty to relieve great distress, as it is not a paramount duty to give pleasure. It would have been my duty to rescue the drowning child at Richmond if I had been there at the time; but it is not, in the same sense, my duty to give Christmas presents to the children of my neighbours. This difference is obscured in the cruder type of utilitarian philosophy which analyses moral goodness in terms of the greatest happiness of the greatest number: but common sense does not ignore it. Common sense knows that fire engines and ambulances are essential services, whereas fun fairs and holiday camps are not. Liberality and kindness are reckoned moral virtues; but they are not moral duties in the sense that the obligation to rescue a drowning child is a moral duty.

It is worth considering the circumstances in which ordinary people find themselves invoking the language of human rights. I suggest they are situations like these:

A black student in South Africa is awarded a scholarship to

Oxford, and then refused a passport by the South African government simply because he is black. We feel this is clear invasion of the human right to freedom of movement. Jews are annihilated by the Nazi government, simply because they are Jews. We feel this is a manifest abuse (an atrocious abuse) of the human right to life. In several countries men are held in prison indefinitely without trial. We feel this is a gross invasion of the human right to liberty and to a fair trial on any criminal charge.

In considering cases of this kind, we are confronted by matters which belong to a totally different moral dimension from questions of social security and holidays with pay. A human right is something of which no one may be deprived without a grave affront to justice. There are certain deeds which should never be done, certain freedoms which should never be invaded, some things which are supremely sacred. If a Declaration of Human Rights is what it purports to be, a declaration of universal moral rights, it should be confined to this sphere of discourse. If rights of another class are introduced, the effect may even be to bring the whole concept of human rights into disrepute. 'It would be a splendid thing', people might say, 'for everyone to have holidays with pay, a splendid thing for everyone to have social security, a splendid thing to have equality before the law, and freedom of speech, and the right to life. One day perhaps, this beautiful ideal may be realised . . .'

Thus the effect of a Universal Declaration which is over-loaded with affirmations of so-called human rights which are not human rights at all is to push *all* talk of human rights out of the clear realm of the morally compelling into the twilight world of utopian aspiration. In the Universal Declaration of 1948 there indeed occurs the phrase 'a common standard of achievement' which brands that Declaration as an attempt to translate rights into ideals. And however else one might choose to define moral rights, they are plainly *not* ideals or aspirations.

Much has been made of the difference between a right and a duty, and the distinction is of course important. But Tom Paine was surely correct when he pointed out that there could be no rights without duties. To speak of a universal right is to speak of a universal duty; to say that all men have a right to life is to impose on all men the duty of respecting human life, to put all men under the same prohibition against attacking, injuring, or endangering the life of any other human being. Indeed, if this universal duty were not imposed, what sense could be made of the concept of a universal human right?

The so-called economic and social rights, insofar as they are intelligible at all, impose no such universal duty. They are rights to be given things, things such as a decent income, schools, and social services. But who is called upon to do the giving? Whose duty is it? When the authors of the United Nations Covenant on Economic and Social Rights assert that 'everyone has the right to social security', are they saying that everyone ought to subscribe to some form of world-wide social security system from which each in turn may benefit in case of need? If something of this kind is meant, why do the United Nations Covenants make no provision for instituting such a system? And if no such system exists, where is the obligation, and where the right? To impose on men a 'duty' which they cannot possibly perform is as absurd in its way, though perhaps not as cruel, as bestowing on them a 'right' which they cannot possibly enjoy.

To deny that the 'economic and social rights' are the universal moral rights of all men is not to deny that they may be the moral rights of some men. In the moral criticism of legal rights, it is certainly arguable that the privileges of some members of a certain community ought to be extended to other members (and perhaps all members) of that community. But this matter is correctly seen as a problem of *socialisation* or *democratisation*—that is, the extension of privileges and immunities—rather than as a problem about the universal rights of all men: and the case for any such specific claims to an extension of legal rights must be argued on other grounds.

When at the time of the French Revolution Babeuf claimed the right of the people to education, he was speaking about the rights of Frenchmen, and not of man. To claim economic and social rights for the members of a given community is a reasonable exercise. And, moreover, in the case of Babeuf, his claim for a popular right to education was fortified by some relevant arguments: he said, rightly or wrongly, that the wealth of

France was produced by the working classes of France, and that those people had therefore earned the right to education. To assert a right which is thus local (i.e., a right of Frenchmen) and earned, is to assert a right which belongs to a different logical category from rights which are universal and not necessarily earned.

It has often been said that a particular man's duties derive from his station: and in a similar way, a particular man's situation in the world will govern the system of rights which he can claim. A miner in Pittsburgh will be able to justify the claim to a great many rights which include some economic and social rights; a miner in Durham will be able to sustain a fairly similar range of rights, but by no means an identical one. A beggar in Calcutta will not be able to produce anything like the same number of just entitlements in the sphere of economic and social benefits; but he has exactly the same rights as the two other men to political and civil rights.

Human rights, indeed, are possessed by the basest criminal. The *New York Times* published not long ago[2] a photograph of the President of the Central African Republic, Monsieur Jean-Bédel Bokassa, in the courtyard of the prison at Bangui. The President was wearing his full regalia, with decorations and medals, and he was personally commanding his soldiers to beat with clubs prisoners who had been convicted of theft. 'Thieves must all die,' he announced. 'There will be no more theft in the Central African Republic.' According to the *New York Times*, 'Of the 46 men beaten, at least three died. Their corpses were put on public display the next day with the battered survivors, many of whom appeared near death.'

This case is peculiarly odious for several reasons. Had the convicts been publicly shot, as were thieves in Nigeria in that same year, the régime could well be accused of employing the kind of cruel and inhuman punishment which is proscribed by Article 5 of the Universal Declaration, but at least the Nigerian régime could quote the practice of eighteenth-century Europe as a precedent for the use of capital punishment for theft. But the President of the Central African Republic could hardly claim to be using punishment at all: the penalty was not one imposed by a court of justice (for the court had already imposed the lawful penalty, imprisonment). What President Bokassa was doing was adding to that penalty a further additional suffering, prescribed by his arbitrary will—the beating to death, or near, of certain convicts—as a means of promoting public order through terror. The smile of the President in the press photographs of the occasion adds one ghoulish refinement to the scene.

Even if such methods *did* protect public order—and the experience of the public shootings of thieves in Nigeria suggests that they do not—the use of torture at the pleasure of a despot is precisely the kind of thing which declarations of the Rights of Man are meant to outlaw, and which the United Nations[3] at its inception was expected to banish from the earth. This is a matter of moral urgency which is far removed from questions of holidays with pay.

IX

The Future of Human Rights

The United Nations Covenant on Economic and Social Rights, which was approved by the General Assembly in 1966, though subsequently ratified by only a few members, is something of a curiosity.[1] It re-states in more cautious language most of the economic and social rights named in the Universal Declaration, and qualifies them in various ways; and, as we have seen, it transfers certain rights from the individual person to what are referred to as 'peoples'. Thus Article One not only states that 'all peoples have the right of self-determination', but further asserts that 'by virtue of that right they freely determine their political status and freely pursue their economic, social, and cultural development'. Here the wording must be considered unfortunate, since it suggests that what is desired is already the case: but Article Two makes it clear that these 'peoples' rights' are not to be understood as universal rights, for section (iii) of that Article asserts: 'Developing countries, with due regard to human rights and their national economy, may determine to what extent they would guarantee the economic rights recognised in the present covenant to non-nationals.' In a later clause of the Covenant, even the right to property (ascribed in the Universal Declaration to individuals) is said to belong to 'peoples': for Article 25 affirms 'the right of *all peoples* [my italics] to enjoy and utilise fully and freely their natural wealth and resources'.

Other clauses in the Covenant, however, ascribe rights to 'everyone', that is to say to individuals. These include the right to work (Article 6), the rights to social security (Article 9), to an adequate standard of living (Article 11), to education (Article 13), and to the 'highest attainable standard of physical and mental health' (Article 12). These are claimed as universal rights. On the other hand, Article 7, by which the 'States

Parties to the present covenant recognise the right of everyone ... to just and favourable conditions of work' implicitly restricts those 'conditions of work' to workers: and it is here that the right to 'periodic holidays with pay' appears together with the right to fair wages, safe and healthy working conditions, equal opportunity for promotion, together with 'rest, leisure, and reasonable limitation of working hours'. In this section, at least, the Covenant has a distinct logical superiority over the Universal Declaration. For it is one thing to claim fair rewards for employees and quite another to ascribe rights to mankind as a whole. Employees have undoubtedly a right to holidays with pay: they earn them: but not all men are employees, and the special rights of employees should not be confused with the common rights of all men.

Even so, the United Nations Covenant is something less than a charter for workers: for though everyone is assured of the right to form trade unions, and the right to strike, that right exists, according to Article 8, only 'provided it is exercised in conformity with the laws of the particular country'. And in any case, the extent to which the United Nations Covenant binds the States Parties adhering to it is minimal. The signatories undertake to submit reports on the measures taken and the progress made in the observance of these rights (Article 16) but no sanctions of any kind are named or contemplated.

Hence although the language of the Covenant is generally of 'binding' nature, the signatories giving 'undertakings' and 'guarantees', its main effect is to reinforce the conception of human rights as ideals or objectives towards which the governments of the world can happily gaze. If the Covenant on Economic and Social Rights had not been associated with the Covenant on Political and Civil Rights it might well have been ratified more widely and more briskly. The thought of Political and Civil Rights is bound to be more disturbing: precisely because the rights it names are universal rights, and rights which claim immediate recognition.

Anyone who studies the activities of the United Nations in the field of human rights since its inception in 1945 is bound to be struck by the extent to which the whole 'Human Rights question' has come to turn more and more on discussions of economic and social rights and less and less on political and civil rights.

There is a political reason for this. Most states could fairly claim that they have pursued some sort of welfare programme since 1945 and even those who have only made the barest efforts in this direction could plausibly claim to be moving, however slowly, towards the objectives named in the Covenant on Economic and Social Rights. Moreover some of the states which have been guilty of the grossest violations of political and civil rights have a respectable record in the matter of welfare legislation. Hence, for their purposes, the more the whole 'Human Rights question' can be transformed into a question about economic and social rights, the better their political ends are served. The example of the Soviet Union is instructive in this respect. Although Russia did not vote in 1948 to support the Universal Declaration, *Pravda* celebrated the anniversary of the Declaration by asserting '. . . in the U.S.S.R. the basic human rights are not only proclaimed, but are guaranteed and consistently implemented.'[2] In Soviet publications of the 1950's the Universal Declaration was described as 'inadequate', but the *Soviet Diplomatic Dictionary* of 1960 gave a more sympathetic, even enthusiastic account of it:

> "The adoption of the Universal Declaration of Human Rights reflected those world-historical changes in international relations which are taking place as a result of the growth of the forces of democracy, peace, and socialism. The imperialist countries were not in a position to ignore the unanimous demand of the peoples on the defence of the rights of the individual and democracy."[3]

The original hostility of the Soviet Union towards the human rights idea at the United Nations was intelligible enough. Marx himself always regarded Declarations of the Rights of Man as products of the bourgeois liberal ideology, which conceived men as isolated competing beings, each possessed of his little empire of rights. Marx preferred to think of man as a *Gattungswesen*, a 'species-being', sharing rights, as he shared duties, with his fellows. The Russians could easily give good Marxist reasons for disapproving of the Universal Declaration of 1948.

Why, then, did they change their posture? The political answer is plainly that the United Nations changed its field of interest. The concept of economic and social rights was as congenial to the Communists as the idea of political and civil rights was alien to them. And the more the economic and social rights were stressed, the more reconciled the Soviet Union became to the idea of human rights as a United Nations activity. Moreover, the idea of economic and social rights proved exceedingly popular in the Third World. The newly independent states which became more and more numerous in the United Nations were preoccupied with two questions above all—the general principle of national independence and practical questions of economic growth. By introducing into the formulation of the human rights question the concept of 'the people'—meaning more or less 'the nation'—in place of the individual human being, the United Nations met these new demands of nationalistic ideology. Furthermore, all the brave new talk about men having a right to a decent standard of living and so forth was useful to representatives of poor countries trying to squeeze economic aid out of rich ones.

The year 1968 was declared by the United Nations to be Human Rights Year, and a large conference of member States was held at Teheran in April and May. The resolutions passed are significant. There was a demand for action against illiteracy, but most of the resolutions concerned imperialist, colonialist, and racist policies in South Africa. There was no motion against the Soviet occupation of the Baltic States, or, indeed, any resolution for which the Soviet Union could not happily vote. There was a resolution demanding the suppression of Nazism and the punishment of war criminals from the Second World War, but no resolution concerning the rights of the Jewish minority in Russia. It was resolved that all remaining overseas European colonies should be freed: but not that East European peoples should have any more independence than they had already.

Could the Soviet Union be accused of violating either the spirit or the letter of Human Rights Year when in the summer of 1968 it sent tanks into Czechoslovakia to suppress the new liberties that Mr Dubcek had conferred on his people? A paradoxical celebration, yes: but one to which the whole momentum of United Nations activity in the Human Rights sphere had, in a sense, been tending. For what the Russians were stamping out in Czechoslovakia in 1968 were not economic and social rights. Social insurance, holidays with pay, and free education continued in Czechoslovakia under Russian occupation as they had before, except perhaps for those professors thrown out of their jobs by the closing of the university, and for writers denied the right to publish and for other silenced intellectuals: but even in their cases the 'right to work' was respected by the offer of manual labour. What was abolished were those political and civil rights which Mr Dubcek had sought at least partially to restore after years of oppression. They were the kind of rights which the Hungarians had sought to achieve by the rising of 1956, which the same Russian tanks had quelled; the rights which some Soviet Jews had sought to vindicate when Stalin liquidated their leaders in 1952.

However, by the 1960's the Soviet Union had little reason to be embarrassed by discussions of the Human Rights question in the United Nations. In 1968 the U.S.S.R. signed both the Covenant on Economic and Social Rights and the Covenant on Political and Civil Rights, though not, of course, the optional protocol to the former covenant which provided for aggrieved individuals to have access to the United Nations Human Rights Commission. Ratification was postponed, but in 1969 the U.S.S.R. formally ratified the International Convention on the Elimination of all forms of Racial Discrimination, and only rejected Article 22, which provides for the reference to the International Court of Justice of disputes between States on the interpretation of the convention. Evidently, the Soviet Union was going to uphold Human Rights only according to its own Soviet conception of human rights. And as that conception, with its emphasis on material satisfaction, gained popularity, the Soviet government was able to transform its image from that of an obvious enemy into that of one of the leading champions of human rights.

And yet it might be thought their signature of the Covenant on Political and Civil Rights would commit the Soviet rulers to at least some greater toleration of political dissent at home. And indeed it did mark a change of policy. After 1968, prominent political dissenters in the U.S.S.R. were not necessarily sent to prison or labour camps: they were put in psychiatric hospitals as prisoners mentally disturbed. When a courageous young Russian named Vladimir Bukovsky[4] revealed this abuse of psychiatry, he was tried and sent to prison with a long-term sentence. But if the Soviet accession to the Covenant on Political and Civil Rights was not taken seriously by the government which signed it, a popular underground movement for civil rights in Russia became increasingly active after 1968. The Soviet government might fool itself into thinking that human rights means holidays with pay and the punishment of war criminals, but ordinary Russian people—like ordinary people of the satellite states—began to demand the rights to life and liberty in unmistakable terms. Year after year at the United Nations, the former Secretary-General U Thant repeated the plea he had made to the representatives of the world's governments during Human Rights Year, 1968, to do something about the implementation of human rights.[5] But just as States delegates at the Teheran Conference preferred to think up new human rights to add to the list rather than confront the problems of enforcing those already named, States members of the United Nations preferred to postpone the measures of 'implementation' entailed by ratification of the Covenants. U Thant retired from the post of Secretary-General of the United Nations with his plea for swift ratification of the Covenants unheard.[6]

The sad thing is that even those Covenants provide only the faintest shadow of an international guarantee of anyone's human rights. One of the things which all the leading theorists of natural rights are agreed about is that natural rights are not absolute. Such rights are founded on natural law and therefore limited by natural law. One conspicuous difference between the Universal Declaration of Human Rights and the United Nations Covenants is that the latter attempt to name the limitations to which human rights are subject. It is fair that they should seek to do so; but the limitations are so extensive that they threaten to take away with one hand what is offered by the other.

Thus, for example, the right of movement is limited by such restrictions as are necessary to protect national security, public safety, health, or morals; the right to freedom of opinion is subject to such restrictions as are 'necessary to protect public safety, order, health, or morals'; the right of assembly is limited by such restrictions as may be 'necessary in a democratic society in the interests of national security or public safety, public order, the protection of public health or morals'.

The wording differs, in ways which may or may not be significant, as between one clause and another of the Covenants. All clauses specify that such restrictions shall be either 'prescribed by law' or be 'in accordance with law'.

Once again we meet some highly ambiguous concepts. First the notion of 'public order' is understood quite differently in different systems of municipal law. Those responsible for drafting the Covenants were, if not very good philosophers, at least lawyers enough to see this when it came to putting the text into two languages:

> 'The English expression "public order" and the French expression *l'ordre public* gave rise to considerable discussion. It was observed that the English expression "public order" was not equivalent to—and indeed was substantially different from—the French expression *l'ordre public* (or the Spanish expression *orden público*). In civil law countries, *l'ordre public* is a legal concept used principally as a basis for negating or restricting private agreements, the exercise of police power or the application of foreign law. In common law countries, the expression "public order" is ordinarily used to mean the absence of public disorder. The common law counterpart of *l'ordre public* is "public policy" rather than "public order." The use of the expression "public order" or *l'ordre public* in the limitations clauses would create uncertainty and might constitute a basis for far-reaching derogations from the rights guaranteed.'[7]

Despite these considerations, the expression remains in the Covenants. The problems it raises are, after all, no greater than those implicit in other expressions in the Covenant, and concerning which the Commission expressed no anxiety. What, for example, is to be made of that phrase which permits limitations on rights 'necessary in a democratic society'? Who is to decide what is necessary for democracy? Again, although there may be professional guidance as to what is necessary to protect public health, there are no experts on public morals.

But perhaps the most unfortunate expression of all is that which allows limitations on men's rights or liberties that are 'prescribed by law' or are 'in accordance with law' or 'lawful'. We have already noted that, so far as positive law is concerned, most invasions of men's rights and liberties *are* lawful. Only the most naive Blackstonian could find any comfort in the requirement that limitations on rights should be lawful; for it is only such as they who can go on believing that anything which is lawful must by definition be just. In their situation a dose of scepticism is a very desirable medicine.

Professor H. L. A. Hart has made this point well:

> 'So long as human beings can gain sufficient co-operation from some to enable them to dominate others, they will use the forms of law as one of their instruments. Wicked men will enact wicked rules which others will enforce. What surely is most needed in order to make men clear-sighted in confronting the official abuse of power is that they should preserve the sense that the certification of something as legally valid is not conclusive to the question of obedience, and that however great the aura of majesty or authority which the official system may have, its demands must in the end be submitted to moral scrutiny. This sense that there is something outside the official system, by reference to which in the last resort the individual must solve his problems of obedience, is surely more likely to be kept alive among those who are accustomed to think that rules of law may be iniquitous than among those who think that nothing iniquitous can anywhere have the status of law.'[8]

Thus, it is not enough to say, in the words of the United Nations Covenants, that rights may be limited by restrictions that are 'lawful'. In those states where human rights are limited to the point of non-existence, those restrictions are perfectly 'lawful' and 'valid' in positive law. The question we have to ask in considering restrictions on human rights is whether those restrictions have the authority of natural law or morality or justice. The Covenants of the United Nations give no indication of this crucial distinction between the two senses of 'law', yet it is upon such a distinction that the whole reality of natural rights rests.

Once more we are led to the question of authority. Who is to decide whether the restrictions on freedom which are valid in positive law in certain places are justifiable in natural law? As things stand, every state is judge in its own cause. There is an obvious need for some impartial body to decide these things, an international court to arbitrate. It is true that the Covenants and the Protocols set up an appellate body, but as it is one to which states alone shall have access, it is of minimal and dubious utility. True, a dozen or more African republics would probably take up the case of the black inhabitants of South Africa. But one can think of many more instances, where no foreign power would interest itself in the fate of an individual whose rights have been invaded, and equally of instances where such a victim would not wish to have his liberty dependent on the intervention of a foreign power. There is indeed something deeply absurd in an arrangement by which something so personal and individual as the rights of man should be settled in committees to which only governments have access; it is a situation worthy of Lewis Carroll.

Of course we cannot expect that men's moral rights shall be the same in all places and at all times. There is a connection between human rights being universal and their formulation being generalised and wide. The basic general principles of morality are minimal precisely because they are universal. Human rights rest on universal principles, but the precise moral rights of men in some communities differ from the precise moral rights of men in other communities, and this is one reason why the formulation of human rights cannot be at the same time closely detailed and of universal application. The moral rights of Englishmen today are not exactly what they were in 1688. Today it is generally agreed in England that the right to liberty entails the right of every adult person to a vote. The right to liberty was not seen in this way in 1688, for then the great illiterate mass of Englishmen neither understood elections nor felt the lack of a vote as a limitation on their freedom.

Similarly today in parts of Switzerland—commonly regarded as one of the most free and most democratic countries—the women have no vote; but so long as the women do not demand the vote and are content with the ancient institution of household suffrage—are content, that is to say, to allow their husbands and fathers to vote in their name—then we cannot say that a natural right is being denied in Switzerland. A right presupposes a claim; if the claim is not made, the question of a right does not arise.

But once the claim *is* made the situation is altered. Even in Switzerland in recent years the demand for women's suffrage has been made, and in several places met. Lauterpächt once wrote of human rights: 'Inasmuch as, upon final analysis, they are an expression of moral claims, they are a powerful lever of legal reform. The moral claims of today are often the legal rights of tomorrow.'[9]

In the advanced, industrialised societies of Europe and North America the claims that are made, and can be reasonably made, by the whole body of inhabitants are considerably greater than could reasonably be made by the majority of people in Asia, Africa, and South America. With industrial progress, one passes from the minimal code of the rights of man to more elaborate rights. But progress should not blind us to the meaning of those minimal rights, for to assert them is to say that no society is so simple that its members can justly be denied them.

To speak of some communities being simpler than others and of more advanced societies having more extended moral rights is perhaps to lay oneself open to misunderstanding. For it is thus that the apologists of *apartheid* speak together with those champions of crude imperialism who say that men of colour can never qualify for the same moral rights as white men. But this is the opposite of the truth. If one believes in moral rights at all, one cannot do less than accept Cecil Rhodes's maxim of equal rights for the equally civilised, and colour is irrelevant to this criterion. It is arguable that the reason why the Republic of South Africa has increasingly alienated the outside world is that it has in recent years so aggressively repudiated Cecil Rhodes. What stirred the Afrikaners to evolve the policy of *apartheid* was not that the black Africans were primitive, but that the black Africans were *ceasing* to be primitive, and beginning to produce an educated class which claimed, and could reasonably claim, equality with the Europeans.

The key document in the history of *apartheid* is the Bantu Education Act, which was designed to close or nationalise the schools in which the Christian missionaries were training an educated African *élite*, and furthermore to shut the doors of the main South African universities to non-European students. In the words of the Minister of Native Affairs: 'There is no place for him [the black African] in the European community above the level of certain humble forms of work.'[10]

Thus the central aim of *apartheid* is to keep the black Africans 'in their place', to halt the process whereby they were becoming as sophisticated and advanced as the Afrikaners, to push them back into tribalism and primitivism. And this, of course, is the very reverse of that policy which was the main moral justification for the existence of the British Empire, namely that the Empire brought backward people forward, educated, trained, and equipped them to live according to the same rule of law by which Englishmen themselves had learned to live.

If rights are to be differently understood in different places, so will there in different places be different limitations placed on the exercise of certain rights. The right to freedom of expression and action is universally limited by the rule that others shall not be injured by anyone's use of his liberty; such use, we say, becomes an 'abuse' of the right to liberty.

A consideration of the limitations which may be placed on human rights is thus as important as an analysis of the rights themselves; otherwise muddle-headed claims for rights are countered by equally muddle-headed arguments about the needs of public order and security. Reason, in the simple sum of reasonableness, is not a bad guide to go by. For example, it is reasonable in many societies to limit the right to marry to persons over sixteen, since this limitation on the right can serve to protect children from injury; but it can never be reasonable to forbid people to marry persons of another race or colour (as is now the law in South Africa), since such an interdiction imposes a useless limitation on freedom. It is reasonable that clubs should exclude candidates disliked by their members, for this is part of the right of privacy; but it is not reasonable that public institutions such as hotels should have a general rule excluding persons of any race.

If the present Irish government has grounds to believe that the free movement of members of the Provisional IRA constitutes a threat to national security, then that government will have a *prima facie* case for controlling those persons' movements; but the South African government's refusal of passports to black African scholars, on the sole grounds that such scholars are black, has no case in reason whatever.

Even so, too much is made of the supposed antithesis between security and freedom. An all-party conference of Privy Councillors on Security which was set up in London after the Burgess and Maclean case produced a report which asserted that 'it is right to continue the practice of tilting the balance in favour of offering greater protection to the security of the state rather than in safeguarding the rights of the individual'. If this is taken at its face value, it is an alarming suggestion. In fact, it was intended to propose something fairly unsensational. The Privy Councillors were concerned with espionage in the Civil Service, and the rule they were laying down was that in borderline cases where a Civil Servant was suspected of some special attachment to the Soviet Union, the traditional rights of the individual Civil Servant should not be upheld at the expense of state security. This did not introduce any very novel principle. Locke, for one, always maintained that toleration could not be extended to people with a prior loyalty to a foreign power. But the wording of the Privy Councillors' report is such that it could easily be read as authorising something more than the imposition of special restrictions on Civil Servants. What makes it ominous is the phrase about 'tilting the balance' in favour of state security against the rights of the individual. For this image of a pair of scales is alien to the whole Western tradition of political liberty. 'Tilting the balance' suggests that the more you push down one side, the side of individual rights, the more the other side, the side of state security, will rise. It is undeniable that the promotion of state security must entail some diminution of individual freedom, but from this it does not follow that the less liberty you have the more security you have, or that any increase in security must bring a corresponding reduction in freedom. In the English-speaking world, it has for generations been the common belief of man that the abridgement of individual rights beyond an extremely limited degree would not only fail to promote the security of the state, but would positively jeopardise the security of the state. Popular scorn for foreign tyrants is not only a matter of disapproval: it stems also from a sense of the folly of the belief that security can be gained by the suppression of liberty.

To claim the traditional rights of man is to claim, among other things, both security *and* liberty. Security is not something which is at odds with human rights, because it is itself a human right; it is nothing other than the right to life re-stated. The security of the individual is bound up with the security of the community; the private enjoyment of the right depends on the common enjoyment of the right. The demand for liberty and security is not the demand for two things which can only with difficulty be balanced or reconciled: it is a demand for two things which naturally belong together. Part of the traditional Western faith in freedom is a belief that a free country is *safer* than an unfree country. History gives us good grounds for continuing to think that this belief is true.

Appendix A

UNIVERSAL DECLARATION
OF HUMAN RIGHTS

PREAMBLE

Whereas recognition of the inherent dignity and of the equal and inalienable rights of all members of the human family is the foundation of freedom, justice and peace in the world,

Whereas disregard and contempt for human rights have resulted in barbarous acts which have outraged the conscience of mankind, and the advent of a world in which human beings shall enjoy freedom of speech and belief and freedom from fear and want has been proclaimed as the highest aspiration of the common people,

Whereas it is essential, if man is not to be compelled to have recourse, as a last resort, to rebellion against tyranny and oppression, that human rights should be protected by the rule of law,

Whereas it is essential to promote the development of friendly relations between nations,

Whereas the peoples of the United Nations have in the Charter reaffirmed their faith in fundamental human rights, in the dignity and worth of the human person and in the equal rights of men and women and have determined to promote social progress and better standards of life in larger freedom,

Whereas Member States have pledged themselves to achieve, in co-operation with the United Nations, the promotion of universal respect for and observance of human rights and fundamental freedoms,

Whereas a common understanding of these rights and freedoms is of the greatest importance for the full realisation of this pledge,

Now, Therefore,

THE GENERAL ASSEMBLY

proclaims

THIS UNIVERSAL DECLARATION OF HUMAN RIGHTS as a common standard of achievement for all peoples and all nations, to the end that every individual and every organ of society, keeping this Declaration constantly in mind, shall strive by teaching and education to promote respect for these rights and freedoms and by progressive measures, national and international, to secure their universal and effective recognition and observance, both among the peoples of Member States themselves and among the peoples of territories under their jurisdiction.

Article 1

All human beings are born free and equal in dignity and rights. They are endowed with reason and conscience and should act towards one another in a spirit of brotherhood.

Article 2

Everyone is entitled to all the rights and freedoms set forth in this Declaration, without distinction of any kind, such as race, colour, sex, language, religion, political or other opinion, national or social origin, property, birth or other status.

Furthermore, no distinction shall be made on the basis of the political, jurisdictional or international status of the country or territory to which a person belongs, whether it be independent, trust, non-self-governing or under any other limitation of sovereignty.

Article 3

Everyone has the right to life, liberty and security of person.

Article 4

No one shall be held in slavery or servitude; slavery and the slave trade shall be prohibited in all their forms.

Article 5

No one shall be subjected to torture or to cruel, inhuman or degrading treatment or punishment.

Article 6

Everyone has the right to recognition everywhere as a person before the law.

Article 7

All are equal before the law and are entitled without any discrimination to equal protection of the law. All are entitled to equal protection against any discrimination in violation of this Declaration and against any incitement to such discrimination.

Article 8

Everyone has the right to an effective remedy by the competent national tribunals for acts violating the fundamental rights granted him by the constitution or by law.

Article 9

No one shall be subjected to arbitrary arrest, detention or exile.

Article 10

Everyone is entitled in full equality to a fair and public hearing by an independent and impartial tribunal, in the determination of his rights and obligations and of any criminal charge against him.

Article 11

(1) Everyone charged with a penal offence has the right to be presumed innocent until proved guilty according to law in a public trial at which he has had all the guarantees necessary for his defence.

(2) No one shall be held guilty of any penal offence on account of any act or omission which did not constitute a penal offence, under national or international law, at the time when it was committed. Nor shall a heavier penalty be imposed than the one that was applicable at the time the penal offence was committed.

Article 12

No one shall be subjected to arbitrary interference with his privacy, family, home or correspondence, nor to attacks upon his honour and reputation. Everyone has the right to the protection of the law against such interference or attacks.

Article 13

(1) Everyone has the right to freedom of movement and residence within the borders of each state.

(2) Everyone has the right to leave any country, including his own, and to return to his country.

Article 14

(1) Everyone has the right to seek and to enjoy in other countries asylum from persecution.

(2) This right may not be invoked in the case of prosecutions genuinely arising from non-political crimes or from acts contrary to the purposes and principles of the United Nations.

Article 15

(1) Everyone has the right to a nationality.

(2) No one shall be arbitrarily deprived of his nationality nor denied the right to change his nationality.

Article 16

(1) Men and women of full age, without any limitation due to race, nationality or religion, have the right to marry and to found a family. They are entitled to equal rights as to marriage, during marriage and at its dissolution.

(2) Marriage shall be entered into only with the free and full consent of the intending spouses.

(3) The family is the natural and fundamental group unit of society and is entitled to protection by society and the State.

Article 17

(1) Everyone has the right to own property alone as well as in association with others.

(2) No one shall be arbitrarily deprived of his property.

Article 18

Everyone has the right to freedom of thought, conscience and religion; this right includes freedom to change his religion or belief, and freedom, either alone or in community with others and in public or private, to manifest his religion or belief in teaching, practice, worship and observance.

Article 19

Everyone has the right to freedom of opinion and expression; this right includes freedom to hold opinions without interference and to seek, receive and impart information and ideas through any media and regardless of frontiers.

Article 20

(1) Everyone has the right to freedom of peaceful assembly and association.

(2) No one may be compelled to belong to an association.

Article 21

(1) Everyone has the right to take part in the government of his country, directly or through freely chosen representatives.

(2) Everyone has the right of equal access to public service in his country.

(3) The will of the people shall be the basis of the authority of government; this will shall be expressed in periodic and genuine elections which shall be by universal and equal suffrage and shall be held by secret vote or by equivalent free voting procedures.

Article 22

Everyone, as a member of society, has the right to social security and is entitled to realisation, through national effort and international co-operation and in accordance with the organisation and resources of each State, of the economic, social and cultural rights indispensable for his dignity and the free development of his personality.

Article 23

(1) Everyone has the right to work, to free choice of employment, to just and favourable conditions of work and to protection against unemployment.

(2) Everyone, without any discrimination, has the right to equal pay for equal work.

(3) Everyone who works has the right to just and favourable remuneration ensuring for himself and his family an existence worthy of human dignity, and supplemented, if necessary, by other means of social protection.

(4) Everyone has the right to form and to join trade unions for the protection of his interests.

Article 24

Everyone has the right to rest and leisure, including reasonable limitation of working hours and periodic holidays with pay.

Article 25

(1) Everyone has the right to a standard of living adequate for the health and well-being of himself and of his family, including food, clothing, housing and medical care and necessary social services, and the right to security in the event of unemployment, sickness, disability, widowhood, old age or other lack of livelihood in circumstances beyond his control.

(2) Motherhood and childhood are entitled to special care and assistance. All children, whether born in or out of wedlock, shall enjoy the same social protection.

Article 26

(1) Everyone has the right to education. Education shall be free, at least in the elementary and fundamental stages. Elementary education shall be compulsory. Technical and professional education shall be made generally available and higher education shall be equally accessible to all on the basis of merit.

(2) Education shall be directed to the full development of the human personality and to the strengthening of respect for human rights and fundamental freedoms. It shall promote

understanding, tolerance and friendship among all nations, racial or religious groups, and shall further the activities of the United Nations for the maintenance of peace.

(3) Parents have a prior right to choose the kind of education that shall be given to their children.

Article 27

(1) Everyone has the right freely to participate in the cultural life of the community, to enjoy the arts and to share in scientific advancement and its benefits.

(2) Everyone has the right to the protection of the moral and material interests resulting from any scientific, literary or artistic production of which he is the author.

Article 28

Everyone is entitled to a social and international order in which the rights and freedoms set forth in this Declaration can be fully realised.

Article 29

(1) Everyone has duties to the community in which alone the free and full development of his personality is possible.

(2) In the exercise of his rights and freedoms, everyone shall be subject only to such limitations as are determined by law solely for the purpose of securing due recognition and respect for the rights and freedoms of others and of meeting the just requirements of morality, public order and the general welfare in a democratic society.

(3) These rights and freedoms may in no case be exercised contrary to the purposes and principles of the United Nations.

Article 30

Nothing in this Declaration may be interpreted as implying for any State, group or person any right to engage in any activity or to perform any act aimed at the destruction of any of the rights and freedoms set forth herein.

Appendix B

INTERNATIONAL COVENANT ON ECONOMIC, SOCIAL AND CULTURAL RIGHTS

PREAMBLE

The States Parties to the present Covenant,

Considering that, in accordance with the principles proclaimed in the Charter of the United Nations, recognition of the inherent dignity and of the equal and inalienable rights of all members of the human family is the foundation of freedom, justice and peace in the world,

Recognising that these rights derive from the inherent dignity of the human person,

Recognising that, in accordance with the Universal Declaration of Human Rights, the ideal of free human beings enjoying freedom from fear and want can only be achieved if conditions are created whereby everyone may enjoy his economic, social and cultural rights, as well as his civil and political rights,

Considering the obligation of States under the Charter of the United Nations to promote universal respect for, and observance of, human rights and freedoms,

Realising that the individual, having duties to other individuals and to the community to which he belongs, is under a responsibility to strive for the promotion and observance of the rights recognised in the present Covenant,

Agree upon the following articles:

PART I

Article 1

1. All peoples have the right of self-determination. By virtue of that right they freely determine their political status and freely pursue their economic, social and cultural development.

2. All peoples may, for their own ends, freely dispose of their natural wealth and resources without prejudice to any obligations arising out of international economic co-operation, based upon the principle of mutual benefit, and international law. In no case may a people be deprived of its own means of subsistence.

3. The States Parties to the present Covenant, including those having responsibility for the administration of Non-Self-Governing and Trust Territories, shall promote the realisation of the right of self-determination, and shall respect that right, in conformity with the provisions of the Charter of the United Nations.

PART II

Article 2

1. Each State Party to the present Covenant undertakes to take steps, individually and through international assistance and co-operation, especially economic and technical, to the maximum of its available resources, with a view to achieving progressively the full realisation of the rights recognised in the present Covenant by all appropriate means, including particularly the adoption of legislative measures.

2. The States Parties to the present Covenant undertake to guarantee that the rights enunciated in the present Covenant will be exercised without discrimination of any kind as to race, colour, sex, language, religion, political or other opinion, national or social origin, property, birth or other status.

3. Developing countries, with due regard to human rights and their national economy, may determine to what extent they would guarantee the economic rights recognised in the present Covenant to non-nationals.

Article 3

The States Parties to the present Covenant undertake to ensure the equal right of men and women to the enjoyment of all economic, social and cultural rights set forth in the present Covenant.

Article 4

The States Parties to the present Covenant recognise that, in the enjoyment of those rights provided by the State in conformity with the present Covenant, the State may subject such rights only to such limitations as are determined by law only in so far as this may be compatible with the nature of these rights and solely for the purpose of promoting the general welfare in a democratic society.

Article 5

1. Nothing in the present Covenant may be interpreted as implying for any State, group or person any right to engage in any activity or to perform any act aimed at the destruction of any of the rights or freedoms recognised herein, or at their limitation to a greater extent than is provided for in the present Covenant.

2. No restriction upon or derogation from any of the fundamental human rights recognised or existing in any country in virtue of law, conventions, regulations or custom shall be admitted on the pretext that the present Covenant does not recognise such rights or that it recognises them to a lesser extent.

PART III

Article 6

1. The States Parties to the present Covenant recognise the right to work, which includes the right of everyone to the opportunity to gain his living by work which he freely chooses or accepts, and will take appropriate steps to safeguard this right.

2. The steps to be taken by a State Party to the present Covenant to achieve the full realisation of this right shall include technical and vocational guidance and training programmes, policies and techniques to achieve steady economic, social and cultural development and full and productive employment under conditions safeguarding fundamental political and economic freedoms to the individual.

Article 7

The States Parties to the present Covenant recognise the right of everyone to the enjoyment of just and favourable conditions of work which ensure, in particular:

(*a*) Remuneration which provides all workers, as a minimum with:

(i) Fair wages and equal remuneration for work of equal value without distinction of any kind, in particular women being guaranteed conditions of work not inferior to those enjoyed by men, with equal pay for equal work;

(ii) A decent living for themselves and their families in accordance with the provisions of the present Covenant;

(*b*) Safe and healthy working conditions;

(*c*) Equal opportunity for everyone to be promoted in his employment to an appropriate higher level, subject to no considerations other than those of seniority and competence;

(*d*) Rest, leisure and reasonable limitation of working hours and periodic holidays with pay, as well as remuneration for public holidays.

Article 8

1. The States Parties to the present Covenant undertake to ensure:

(*a*) The right of everyone to form trade unions and join the trade union of his choice, subject only to the rules of the organisation concerned, for the promotion and protection of his economic and social interests. No restrictions may be placed on the exercise of this right other than those prescribed by law and which are necessary in a democratic society in the interests of national security or public order or for the protection of the rights and freedoms of others;

(*b*) The right of trade unions to establish national federations or confederations and the right of the latter to form or join international trade-union organisations;

(*c*) The right of trade unions to function freely subject to no limitations other than those prescribed by law and which are necessary in a democratic society in the interests of national security or public order or for the protection of the rights and freedoms of others;

(*d*) The right to strike, provided that it is exercised in conformity with the laws of the particular country.

2. This article shall not prevent the imposition of lawful restrictions on the exercise of these rights by members of the armed forces or of the police or of the administration of the State.

3. Nothing in this article shall authorise States Parties to the International Labour Organisation Convention of 1948 concerning Freedom of Association and Protection of the Right to Organise to take legislative measures which would prejudice, or apply the law in such a manner as would prejudice, the guarantees provided for in that Convention.

Article 9

The States Parties to the present Covenant recognise the right of everyone to social security, including social insurance.

Article 10

The States Parties to the present Covenant recognise that:

1. The widest possible protection and assistance should be accorded to the family, which is the natural and fundamental group unit of society, particularly for its establishment and while it is responsible for the care and education of dependent children. Marriage must be entered into with the free consent of the intending spouses.

2. Special protection should be accorded to mothers during a reasonable period before and after childbirth. During such period working mothers should be accorded paid leave or leave with adequate social security benefits.

3. Special measures of protection and assistance should be taken on behalf of all children and young persons without any discrimination for reasons of parentage or other conditions. Children and young persons should be protected from economic and social exploitation. Their employment in work harmful to their morals or health or dangerous to life or likely to hamper their normal development should be punishable by law. States should also set age limits below which the paid employment of child labour should be prohibited and punishable by law.

Article 11

1. The States Parties to the present Covenant recognise the right of everyone to an adequate standard of living for himself and his family, including adequate food, clothing and housing, and to the continuous improvement of living conditions. The States Parties will take appropriate steps to ensure the realisation of this right, recognising to this effect the essential importance of international co-operation based on free consent.

2. The States Parties to the present Covenant, recognising the fundamental right of everyone to be free from hunger, shall take, individually and through international co-operation, the measures, including specific programmes, which are needed:

(*a*) To improve methods of production, conservation and distribution of food by making full use of technical and scientific knowledge, by disseminating knowledge of the principles of nutrition and by developing or reforming agrarian systems in such a way as to achieve the most efficient development and utilisation of natural resources;

(*b*) Taking into account the problems of both food-importing and food-exporting countries, to ensure an equitable distribution of world food supplies in relation to need.

Article 12

1. The States Parties to the present Covenant recognise the right of everyone to the enjoyment of the highest attainable standard of physical and mental health.

2. The steps to be taken by the States Parties to the present Covenant to achieve the full realisation of this right shall include those necessary for:

(*a*) The provision for the reduction of the stillbirth-rate and of infant mortality and for the healthy development of the child;

(*b*) The improvement of all aspects of environmental and industrial hygiene;

(*c*) The prevention, treatment and control of epidemic, endemic, occupational and other diseases;

(*d*) The creation of conditions which would assure to all medical service and medical attention in the event of sickness.

Article 13

1. The States Parties to the present Covenant recognise the right of everyone to education. They agree that education shall be directed to the full development of the human personality and the sense of its dignity, and shall strengthen the respect for human rights and fundamental freedoms. They further agree that education shall enable all persons to participate effectively in a free society, promote understanding, tolerance and friendship among all nations and all racial, ethnic or religious groups, and further the activities of the United Nations for the maintenance of peace.

2. The States Parties to the present Covenant recognise that, with a view to achieving the full realisation of this right:

(*a*) Primary education shall be compulsory and available free to all;

(*b*) Secondary education in its different forms, including technical and vocational secondary education, shall be made generally available and accessible to all by every appropriate means, and in particular by the progressive introduction of free education;

(*c*) Higher education shall be made equally accessible to all, on the basis of capacity, by every appropriate means, and in particular by the progressive introduction of free education;

(*d*) Fundamental education shall be encouraged or intensified as far as possible for those persons who have not received or completed the whole period of their primary education;

(*e*) The development of a system of schools at all levels shall be actively pursued, an adequate fellowship system shall be established, and the material conditions of teaching staff shall be continuously improved.

3. The States Parties to the present Covenant undertake to have respect for the liberty of parents and, when applicable, legal guardians to choose for their children schools, other than those established by the public authorities, which conform to such minimum educational standards as may be laid down or approved by the State and to ensure the religious and moral education of their children in conformity with their own convictions.

4. No part of this article shall be construed so as to interfere with the liberty of individuals and bodies to establish and direct educational institutions, subject always to the observance of the principles set forth in paragraph 1 of this article and to the requirement that the education given in such institutions shall conform to such minimum standards as may be laid down by the State.

Article 14

Each State Party to the present Covenant which, at the time of becoming a Party, has not been able to secure in its metropolitan territory or other territories under its jurisdiction compulsory primary education, free of charge, undertakes, within two years, to work out and adopt a detailed plan of action for the progressive implementation, within a reasonable number of years, to be fixed in the plan, of the principle of compulsory education free of charge for all.

Article 15

1. The States Parties to the present Covenant recognise the right of everyone:

(*a*) To take part in cultural life;

(*b*) To enjoy the benefits of scientific progress and its applications;

(*c*) To benefit from the protection of the moral and material interests resulting from any scientific, literary or artistic production of which he is the author.

2. The steps to be taken by the States Parties to the present Covenant to achieve the full realisation of this right shall include those necessary for the conservation, the development and the diffusion of science and culture.

3. The States Parties to the present Covenant undertake to respect the freedom indispensable for scientific research and creative activity.

4. The States Parties to the present Covenant recognise the benefits to be derived from the encouragement and development of international contacts and co-operation in the scientific and cultural fields.

PART IV

Article 16

1. The States Parties to the present Covenant undertake to submit in conformity with this part of the Covenant reports on the measures which they have adopted and the progress made in achieving the observance of the rights recognised herein.

2. (a) All reports shall be submitted to the Secretary-General of the United Nations, who shall transmit copies to the Economic and Social Council for consideration in accordance with the provisions of the present Covenant;

(b) The Secretary-General of the United Nations shall also transmit to the specialised agencies copies of the reports, or any relevant parts therefrom, from States Parties to the present Covenant which are also members of these specialised agencies in so far as these reports, or parts therefrom, relate to any matters which fall within the responsibilities of the said agencies in accordance with their constitutional instruments.

Article 17

1. The States Parties to the present Covenant shall furnish their reports in stages, in accordance with a programme to be established by the Economic and Social Council within one year of the entry into force of the present Covenant after consultation with the States Parties and the specialised agencies concerned.

2. Reports may indicate factors and difficulties affecting the degree of fulfilment of obligations under the present Covenant.

3. Where relevant information has previously been furnished to the United Nations or to any specialised agency by any State Party to the present Covenant, it will not be necessary to reproduce that information, but a precise reference to the information so furnished will suffice.

Article 18

Pursuant to its responsibilities under the Charter of the United Nations in the field of human rights and fundamental freedoms, the Economic and Social Council may make arrangements with the specialised agencies in respect of their reporting to it on the progress made in achieving the observance of the provisions of the present Covenant falling within the scope of their activities. These reports may include particulars of decisions and recommendations on such implementation adopted by their competent organs.

Article 19

The Economic and Social Council may transmit to the Commission on Human Rights for study and general recommendation or, as appropriate, for information the reports concerning human rights submitted by States in accordance with articles 16 and 17, and those concerning human rights submitted by the specialised agencies in accordance with article 18.

Article 20

The States Parties to the present Covenant and the specialised agencies concerned may submit comments to the Economic and Social Council on any general recommendation under article 19 or reference to such general recommendation in any report of the Commission on Human Rights or any documentation referred to therein.

Article 21

The Economic and Social Council may submit from time to time to the General Assembly reports with recommendations of a general nature and a summary of the information received from the States Parties to the present Covenant and the specialised agencies on the measures taken and the progress made in achieving general observance of the rights recognised in the present Covenant.

Article 22

The Economic and Social Council may bring to the attention of other organs of the United Nations, their subsidiary organs and specialised agencies concerned with furnishing technical assistance any matters arising out of the reports referred to in this part of the present Covenant which may assist such bodies in deciding, each within its field of competence, on the advisability of international measures likely to contribute to the effective progressive implementation of the present Covenant.

Article 23

The States Parties to the present Covenant agree that international action for the achievement of the rights recognised in the present Covenant includes such methods as the conclusion of conventions, the adoption of recommendations, the furnishing of technical assistance and the holding of regional meetings and technical meetings for the purpose of consultation and study organised in conjunction with the Governments concerned.

Article 24

Nothing in the present Covenant shall be interpreted as impairing the provisions of the Charter of the United Nations and of the constitutions of the specialised agencies which define the respective responsibilities of the various organs of the United Nations and of the specialised agencies in regard to the matters dealt with in the present Covenant.

Article 25

Nothing in the present Covenant shall be interpreted as impairing the inherent right of all peoples to enjoy and utilise fully and freely their natural wealth and resources.

PART V

Article 26

1. The present Covenant is open for signature by any State Member of the United Nations or member of any of its specialised agencies, by any State Party to the Statute of the International Court of Justice, and by any other State which has been invited by the General Assembly of the United Nations to become a party to the present Covenant.

2. The present Covenant is subject to ratification. Instruments of ratification shall be deposited with the Secretary-General of the United Nations.

3. The present Covenant shall be open to accession by any State referred to in paragraph 1 of this article.

4. Accession shall be effected by the deposit of an instrument of accession with the Secretary-General of the United Nations.

5. The Secretary-General of the United Nations shall inform all States which have signed the present Covenant or acceded to it of the deposit of each instrument of ratification or accession.

Article 27

1. The present Covenant shall enter into force three months after the date of the deposit with the Secretary-General of the United Nations of the thirty-fifth instrument of ratification or instrument of accession.

2. For each State ratifying the present Covenant or acceding to it after the deposit of the thirty-fifth instrument of ratification or instrument of accession, the present Covenant shall enter into force three months after the date of the deposit of its own instrument of ratification or instrument of accession.

Article 28

The provisions of the present Covenant shall extend to all parts of federal States without any limitations or exceptions.

Article 29

1. Any State Party to the present Covenant may propose an amendment and file it with the Secretary-General of the United Nations. The Secretary-General shall thereupon communicate any proposed amendments to the States Parties to the present Covenant with a request that they notify him whether they favour a conference of States Parties for the purpose of considering and voting upon the proposals. In the event that at least one third of the States Parties favours such a conference, the Secretary-General shall convene the conference under the auspices of the United Nations. Any amendment adopted by a majority of the States Parties present and voting at the conference shall be submitted to the General Assembly of the United Nations for approval.

2. Amendments shall come into force when they have been approved by the General Assembly of the United Nations and accepted by a two-thirds majority of the States Parties to

the present Covenant in accordance with their respective constitutional processes.

3. When amendments come into force they shall be binding on those States Parties which have accepted them, other States Parties still being bound by the provisions of the present Covenant and any earlier amendment which they have accepted.

Article 30

Irrespective of the notifications made under article 26, paragraph 5, the Secretary-General of the United Nations shall inform all States referred to in paragraph 1 of the same article of the following particulars:

(*a*) Signatures, ratifications and accessions under article 26;

(*b*) The date of the entry into force of the present Covenant under article 27 and the date of the entry into force of any amendments under article 29.

Article 31

1. The present Covenant, of which the Chinese, English, French, Russian and Spanish texts are equally authentic, shall be deposited in the archives of the United Nations.

2. The Secretary-General of the United Nations shall transmit certified copies of the present Covenant to all States referred to in article 26.

INTERNATIONAL COVENANT ON CIVIL AND POLITICAL RIGHTS

PREAMBLE

The States Parties to the present Covenant,

Considering that, in accordance with the principles proclaimed in the Charter of the United Nations, recognition of the inherent dignity and of the equal and inalienable rights of all members of the human family is the foundation of freedom, justice and peace in the world,

Recognising that these rights derive from the inherent dignity of the human person,

Recognising that, in accordance with the Universal Declaration of Human Rights, the ideal of free human beings enjoying civil and political freedom and freedom from fear and want can only be achieved if conditions are created whereby everyone may enjoy his civil and political rights, as well as his economic, social and cultural rights,

Considering the obligation of States under the Charter of the United Nations to promote universal respect for, and observance of, human rights and freedoms,

Realising that the individual, having duties to other individuals and to the community to which he belongs, is under a responsibility to strive for the promotion and observance of the rights recognised in the present Covenant,

Agree upon the following articles:

PART I

Article 1

1. All peoples have the right of self-determination. By virtue of that right they freely determine their political status and freely pursue their economic, social and cultural development.

2. All peoples may, for their own ends, freely dispose of their natural wealth and resources without prejudice to any obligations arising out of international economic co-operation, based upon the principle of mutual benefit, and international law. In no case may a people be deprived of its own means of subsistence.

3. The States Parties to the present Covenant, including those having responsibility for the administration of Non-Self-Governing and Trust Territories, shall promote the realisation of the right of self-determination, and shall respect that right, in conformity with the provisions of the Charter of the United Nations.

PART II

Article 2

1. Each State Party to the present Covenant undertakes to respect and to ensure to all individuals within its territory

and subject to its jurisdiction the rights recognised in the present Covenant, without distinction of any kind, such as race, colour, sex, language, religion, political or other opinion, national or social origin, property, birth or other status.

2. Where not already provided for by existing legislative or other measures, each State Party to the present Covenant undertakes to take the necessary steps, in accordance with its constitutional processes and with the provisions of the present Covenant, to adopt such legislative or other measures as may be necessary to give effect to the rights recognised in the present Covenant.

3. Each State Party to the present Covenant undertakes:

(a) To ensure that any person whose rights or freedoms as herein recognised are violated shall have an effective remedy, notwithstanding that the violation has been committed by persons acting in an official capacity;

(b) To ensure that any person claiming such a remedy shall have his right thereto determined by competent judicial, administrative or legislative authorities, or by any other competent authority provided for by the legal system of the State, and to develop the possibilities of judicial remedy;

(c) To ensure that the competent authorities shall enforce such remedies when granted.

Article 3

The States Parties to the present Covenant undertake to ensure the equal right of men and women to the enjoyment of all civil and political rights set forth in the present Covenant.

Article 4

1. In time of public emergency which threatens the life of the nation and the existence of which is officially proclaimed, the States Parties to the present Covenant may take measures derogating from their obligations under the present Covenant to the extent strictly required by the exigencies of the situation, provided that such measures are not inconsistent with their other obligations under international law and do not involve discrimination solely on the ground of race, colour, sex, language, religion or social origin.

2. No derogation from articles 6, 7, 8 (paragraphs 1 and 2), 11, 15, 16 and 18 may be made under this provision.

3. Any State Party to the present Covenant availing itself of the right of derogation shall immediately inform the other States Parties to the present Covenant, through the intermediary of the Secretary-General of the United Nations, of the provisions from which it has derogated and of the reasons by which it was actuated. A further communication shall be made, through the same intermediary, on the date on which it terminates such derogation.

Article 5

1. Nothing in the present Covenant may be interpreted as implying for any State, group or person any right to engage in any activity or perform any act aimed at the destruction of any of the rights and freedoms recognised herein or at their limitation to a greater extent than is provided for in the present Covenant.

2. There shall be no restriction upon or derogation from any of the fundamental human rights recognised or existing in any State Party to the present Covenant pursuant to law, conventions, regulations or custom on the pretext that the present Covenant does not recognise such rights or that it recognises them to a lesser extent.

PART III

Article 6

1. Every human being has the inherent right to life. This right shall be protected by law. No one shall be arbitrarily deprived of his life.

2. In countries which have not abolished the death penalty, sentence of death may be imposed only for the most serious crimes in accordance with the law in force at the time of the commission of the crime and not contrary to the provisions of the present Covenant and to the Convention on the Prevention and Punishment of the Crime of Genocide. This penalty can only be carried out pursuant to a final judgement rendered by a competent court.

3. When deprivation of life constitutes the crime of genocide, it is understood that nothing in this article shall authorise any State Party to the present Covenant to derogate in any way from any obligation assumed under the provisions of the Convention on the Prevention and Punishment of the Crime of Genocide.

4. Anyone sentenced to death shall have the right to seek pardon or commutation of the sentence. Amnesty, pardon or commutation of the sentence of death may be granted in all cases.

5. Sentence of death shall not be imposed for crimes committed by persons below eighteen years of age and shall not be carried out on pregnant women.

6. Nothing in this article shall be invoked to delay or to prevent the abolition of capital punishment by any State Party to the present Covenant.

Article 7

No one shall be subjected to torture or to cruel, inhuman or degrading treatment or punishment. In particular, no one shall be subjected without his free consent to medical or scientific experimentation.

Article 8

1. No one shall be held in slavery; slavery and the slave-trade in all their forms shall be prohibited.

2. No one shall be held in servitude.

3. (a) No one shall be required to perform forced or compulsory labour;

(b) Paragraph 3 (a) shall not be held to preclude, in countries where imprisonment with hard labour may be imposed as a punishment for a crime, the performance of hard labour in pursuance of a sentence to such punishment by a competent court;

(c) For the purpose of this paragraph the term 'forced or compulsory labour' shall not include:

(i) Any work or service, not referred to in sub-paragraph (b), normally required of a person who is under detention in consequence of a lawful order of a court, or of a person during conditional release from such detention;

(ii) Any service of a military character and, in countries where conscientious objection is recognised, any national service required by law of conscientious objectors;

(iii) Any service exacted in cases of emergency or calamity threatening the life or well-being of the community;

(iv) Any work or service which forms part of normal civil obligations.

Article 9

1. Everyone has the right to liberty and security of person. No one shall be subjected to arbitrary arrest or detention. No one shall be deprived of his liberty except on such grounds and in accordance with such procedure as are established by law.

2. Anyone who is arrested shall be informed, at the time of arrest, of the reasons for his arrest and shall be promptly informed of any charges against him.

3. Anyone arrested or detained on a criminal charge shall be brought promptly before a judge or other officer authorised by law to exercise judicial power and shall be entitled to trial within a reasonable time or to release. It shall not be the general rule that persons awaiting trial shall be detained in custody, but release may be subject to guarantees to appear for trial, at any other stage of the judicial proceedings, and, should occasion arise, for execution of the judgement.

4. Anyone who is deprived of his liberty by arrest or detention shall be entitled to take proceedings before a court, in order that that court may decide without delay on the lawfulness of his detention and order his release if the detention is not lawful.

5. Anyone who has been the victim of unlawful arrest or detention shall have an enforceable right to compensation.

Article 10

1. All persons deprived of their liberty shall be treated with humanity and with respect for the inherent dignity of the human person.

2. (*a*) Accused persons shall, save in exceptional circumstances, be segregated from convicted persons and shall be subject to separate treatment appropriate to their status as unconvicted persons;

(*b*) Accused juvenile persons shall be separated from adults and brought as speedily as possible for adjudication.

3. The penitentiary system shall comprise treatment of prisoners the essential aim of which shall be their reformation and social rehabilitation. Juvenile offenders shall be segregated from adults and be accorded treatment appropriate to their age and legal status.

Article 11

No one shall be imprisoned merely on the ground of inability to fulfil a contractual obligation.

Article 12

1. Everyone lawfully within the territory of a State shall, within that territory, have the right to liberty of movement and freedom to choose his residence.

2. Everyone shall be free to leave any country, including his own.

3. The above-mentioned rights shall not be subject to any restrictions except those which are provided by law, are necessary to protect national security, public order (*ordre public*), public health or morals or the rights and freedoms of others, and are consistent with the other rights recognised in the present Covenant.

4. No one shall be arbitrarily deprived of the right to enter his own country.

Article 13

An alien lawfully in the territory of a State Party to the present Covenant may be expelled therefrom only in pursuance of a decision reached in accordance with law and shall, except where compelling reasons of national security otherwise require, be allowed to submit the reasons against his expulsion and to have his case reviewed by, and be represented for the purpose before, the competent authority or a person or persons especially designated by the competent authority.

Article 14

1. All persons shall be equal before the courts and tribunals. In the determination of any criminal charge against him, or of his rights and obligations in a suit at law, everyone shall be entitled to a fair and public hearing by a competent, independent and impartial tribunal established by law. The Press and the public may be excluded from all or part of a trial for reasons of morals, public order (*ordre public*) or national security in a democratic society, or when the interest of the private lives of the parties so requires, or to the extent strictly necessary in the opinion of the court in special circumstances where publicity would prejudice the interests of justice; but any judgement rendered in a criminal case or in a suit at law shall be made public except where the interest of juvenile persons otherwise requires or the proceedings concern matrimonial disputes or the guardianship of children.

2. Everyone charged with a criminal offence shall have the right to be presumed innocent until proved guilty according to law.

3. In the determination of any criminal charge against him, everyone shall be entitled to the following minimum guarantees, in full equality:

(*a*) To be informed promptly and in detail in a language which he understands of the nature and cause of the charge against him;

(*b*) To have adequate time and facilities for the preparation of his defence and to communicate with counsel of his own choosing;

(*c*) To be tried without undue delay;

(*d*) To be tried in his presence, and to defend himself in person or through legal assistance of his own choosing; to be informed, if he does not have legal assistance, of this right; and to have legal assistance assigned to him, in any case where the interests of justice so require, and without payment by him in any such case if he does not have sufficient means to pay for it;

(*e*) To examine, or have examined, the witnesses against him and to obtain the attendance and examination of witnesses on his behalf under the same conditions as witnesses against him;

(*f*) To have the free assistance of an interpreter if he cannot understand or speak the language used in court;

(*g*) Not to be compelled to testify against himself or to confess guilt.

4. In the case of juvenile persons, the procedure shall be such as will take account of their age and the desirability of promoting their rehabilitation.

5. Everyone convicted of a crime shall have the right to his conviction and sentence being reviewed by a higher tribunal according to law.

6. When a person has by a final decision been convicted of a criminal offence and when subsequently his conviction has been reversed or he has been pardoned on the ground that a new or newly discovered fact shows conclusively that there has been a miscarriage of justice, the person who has suffered punishment as a result of such conviction shall be compensated according to law, unless it is proved that the non-disclosure of the unknown fact in time is wholly or partly attributable to him.

7. No one shall be liable to be tried or punished again for an offence for which he has already been finally convicted or acquitted in accordance with the law and penal procedure of each country.

Article 15

1. No one shall be held guilty of any criminal offence on account of any act or omission which did not constitute a criminal offence, under national or international law, at the time when it was committed. Nor shall a heavier penalty be imposed than the one that was applicable at the time when the criminal offence was committed. If, subsequent to the commission of the offence, provision is made by law for the imposition of a lighter penalty, the offender shall benefit thereby.

2. Nothing in this article shall prejudice the trial and

punishment of any person for any act or omission which, at the time when it was committed, was criminal according to the general principles of law recognised by the community of nations.

Article 16

Everyone shall have the right to recognition everywhere as a person before the law.

Article 17

1. No one shall be subjected to arbitrary or unlawful interference with his privacy, family, home or correspondence, nor to unlawful attacks on his honour and reputation.

2. Everyone has the right to the protection of the law against such interference or attacks.

Article 18

1. Everyone shall have the right to freedom of thought, conscience and religion. This right shall include freedom to have or to adopt a religion or belief of his choice, and freedom, either individually or in community with others and in public or private, to manifest his religion or belief in worship, observance, practice and teaching.

2. No one shall be subject to coercion which would impair his freedom to have or to adopt a religion or belief of his choice.

3. Freedom to manifest one's religion or beliefs may be subject only to such limitations as are prescribed by law and are necessary to protect public safety, order, health, or morals or the fundamental rights and freedoms of others.

4. The States Parties to the present Covenant undertake to have respect for the liberty of parents and, when applicable, legal guardians to ensure the religious and moral education of their children in conformity with their own convictions.

Article 19

1. Everyone shall have the right to hold opinions without interference.

2. Everyone shall have the right to freedom of expression; this right shall include freedom to seek, receive and impart information and ideas of all kinds, regardless of frontiers, either orally, in writing or in print, in the form of art, or through any other media of his choice.

3. The exercise of the rights provided for in paragraph 2 of this article carries with it special duties and responsibilities. It may therefore be subject to certain restrictions, but these shall only be such as are provided by law and are necessary:

(*a*) For respect of the rights or reputations of others;

(*b*) For the protection of national security or of public order (*ordre public*), or of public health or morals.

Article 20

1. Any propaganda for war shall be prohibited by law.

2. Any advocacy of national, racial or religious hatred that constitutes incitement to discrimination, hostility or violence shall be prohibited by law.

Article 21

The right of peaceful assembly shall be recognised. No restrictions may be placed on the exercise of this right other than those imposed in conformity with the law and which are necessary in a democratic society in the interests of national security or public safety, public order (*ordre public*), the protection of public health or morals or the protection of the rights and freedoms of others.

Article 22

1. Everyone shall have the right to freedom of association with others, including the right to form and join trade unions for the protection of his interests.

2. No restrictions may be placed on the exercise of this right other than those which are prescribed by law and which are necessary in a democratic society in the interests of national security or public safety, public order (*ordre public*), the protection of public health or morals or the protection of the rights and freedoms of others. This article shall not

prevent the imposition of lawful restrictions on members of the armed forces and of the police in their exercise of this right.

3. Nothing in this article shall authorise States Parties to the International Labour Organisation Convention of 1948 concerning Freedom of Association and Protection of the Right to Organise to take legislative measures which would prejudice, or to apply the law in such a manner as to prejudice, the guarantees provided for in that Convention.

Article 23

1. The family is the natural and fundamental group unit of society and is entitled to protection by society and the State.

2. The right of men and women of marriageable age to marry and to found a family shall be recognised.

3. No marriage shall be entered into without the free and full consent of the intending spouses.

4. States Parties to the present Covenant shall take appropriate steps to ensure equality of rights and responsibilities of spouses as to marriage, during marriage and at its dissolution. In the case of dissolution, provision shall be made for the necessary protection of any children.

Article 24

1. Every child shall have, without any discrimination as to race, colour, sex, language, religion, national or social origin, property or birth, the right to such measures of protection as are required by his status as a minor, on the part of his family, society and the State.

2. Every child shall be registered immediately after birth and shall have a name.

3. Every child has the right to acquire a nationality.

Article 25

Every citizen shall have the right and the opportunity, without any of the distinctions mentioned in article 2 and without unreasonable restrictions:

(a) To take part in the conduct of public affairs, directly or through freely chosen representatives;

(*b*) To vote and to be elected at genuine periodic elections which shall be by universal and equal suffrage and shall be held by secret ballot, guaranteeing the free expression of the will of the electors;

(*c*) To have access, on general terms of equality, to public service in his country.

Article 26

All persons are equal before the law and are entitled without any discrimination to the equal protection of the law. In this respect, the law shall prohibit any discrimination and guarantee to all persons equal and effective protection against discrimination on any ground such as race, colour, sex, language, religion, political or other opinion, national or social origin, property, birth or other status.

Article 27

In those States in which ethnic, religious or linguistic minorities exist, persons belonging to such minorities shall not be denied the right, in community with the other members of their group, to enjoy their own culture, to profess and practice their own religion, or to use their own language.

PART IV

Article 28

1. There shall be established a Human Rights Committee (hereafter referred to in the present Covenant as the Committee). It shall consist of eighteen members and shall carry out the functions hereinafter provided.

2. The Committee shall be composed of nationals of the States Parties to the present Covenant who shall be persons of high moral character and recognised competence in the field of human rights, consideration being given to the usefulness of the participation of some persons having legal experience.

3. The members of the Committee shall be elected and shall serve in their personal capacity.

Article 29

1. The members of the Committee shall be elected by secret ballot from a list of persons possessing the qualifications prescribed in article 28 and nominated for the purpose by the States Parties to the present Covenant.

2. Each State Party to the present Covenant may nominate not more than two persons. These persons shall be nationals of the nominating State.

3. A person shall be eligible for renomination.

Article 30

1. The initial election shall be held no later than six months after the date of the entry into force of the present Covenant.

2. At least four months before the date of each election to the Committee, other than an election to fill a vacancy declared in accordance with article 34, the Secretary-General of the United Nations shall address a written invitation to the States Parties to the present Covenant to submit their nominations for membership of the Committee within three months.

3. The Secretary-General of the United Nations shall prepare a list in alphabetical order of all the persons thus nominated, with an indication of the States Parties which have nominated them, and shall submit it to the States Parties to the present Covenant no later than one month before the date of each election.

4. Elections of the members of the Committee shall be held at a meeting of the States Parties to the present Covenant convened by the Secretary-General of the United Nations at the Headquarters of the United Nations. At that meeting, for which two thirds of the States Parties to the present Covenant shall constitute a quorum, the persons elected to the Committee shall be those nominees who obtain the largest number of votes and an absolute majority of the votes of the representatives of States Parties present and voting.

Article 31

1. The Committee may not include more than one national of the same State.

2. In the election of the Committee, consideration shall be given to equitable geographical distribution of membership and to the representation of the different forms of civilisation and of the principal legal systems.

Article 32

1. The members of the Committee shall be elected for a term of four years. They shall be eligible for re-election if renominated. However, the terms of nine of the members elected at the first election shall expire at the end of two years; immediately after the first election, the names of these nine members shall be chosen by lot by the Chairman of the meeting referred to in article 30, paragraph 4.

2. Elections at the expiry of office shall be held in accordance with the preceding articles of this part of the present Covenant.

Article 33

1. If, in the unanimous opinion of the other members, a member of the Committee has ceased to carry out his functions for any cause other than absence of a temporary character, the Chairman of the Committee shall notify the Secretary-General of the United Nations, who shall then declare the seat of that member to be vacant.

2. In the event of the death or the resignation of a member of the Committee, the Chairman shall immediately notify the Secretary-General of the United Nations, who shall declare the seat vacant from the date of death or the date on which the resignation takes effect.

Article 34

1. When a vacancy is declared in accordance with article 33 and if the term of office of the member to be replaced does not expire within six months of the declaration of the vacancy, the Secretary-General of the United Nations shall notify each of the States Parties to the present Covenant, which may within two months submit nominations in accordance with article 29 for the purpose of filling the vacancy.

2. The Secretary-General of the United Nations shall

prepare a list in alphabetical order of the persons thus nominated and shall submit it to the States Parties to the present Covenant. The election to fill the vacancy shall then take place in accordance with the relevant provisions of this part of the present Covenant.

3. A member of the Committee elected to fill a vacancy declared in accordance with article 33 shall hold office for the remainder of the term of the member who vacated the seat on the Committee under the provisions of that article.

Article 35

The members of the Committee shall, with the approval of the General Assembly of the United Nations, receive emoluments from United Nations resources on such terms and conditions as the General Assembly may decide, having regard to the importance of the Committee's responsibilities.

Article 36

The Secretary-General of the United Nations shall provide the necessary staff and facilities for the effective performance of the functions of the Committee under the present Covenant.

Article 37

1. The Secretary-General of the United Nations shall convene the initial meeting of the Committee at the Headquarters of the United Nations.

2. After its initial meeting, the Committee shall meet at such times as shall be provided in its rules of procedure.

3. The Committee shall normally meet at the Headquarters of the United Nations or at the United Nations Office at Geneva.

Article 38

Every member of the Committee shall, before taking up his duties, make a solemn declaration in open committee that he will perform his functions impartially and conscientiously.

Article 39

1. The Committee shall elect its officers for a term of two years. They may be re-elected.

2. The Committee shall establish its own rules of procedure, but these rules shall provide, *inter alia*, that:

(*a*) Twelve members shall constitute a quorum;

(*b*) Decisions of the Committee shall be made by a majority vote of the members present.

Article 40

1. The States Parties to the present Covenant undertake to submit reports on the measures they have adopted which give effect to the rights recognised herein and on the progress made in the enjoyment of those rights:

(*a*) Within one year of the entry into force of the present Covenant for the States Parties concerned;

(*b*) Thereafter whenever the Committee so requests.

2. All reports shall be submitted to the Secretary-General of the United Nations, who shall transmit them to the Committee for consideration. Reports shall indicate the factors and difficulties, if any, affecting the implementation of the present Covenant.

3. The Secretary-General of the United Nations may, after consultation with the Committee, transmit to the specialised agencies concerned copies of such parts of the reports as may fall within their field of competence.

4. The Committee shall study the reports submitted by the States Parties to the present Covenant. It shall transmit its reports, and such general comments as it may consider appropriate, to the States Parties. The Committee may also transmit to the Economic and Social Council these comments along with the copies of the reports it has received from States Parties to the present Covenant.

5. The States Parties to the present Covenant may submit to the Committee observations on any comments that may be made in accordance with paragraph 4 of this article.

Article 41

1. A State Party to the present Covenant may at any time declare under this article that it recognises the competence of

the Committee to receive and consider communications to the effect that a State Party claims that another State Party is not fulfilling its obligations under the present Covenant. Communications under this article may be received and considered only if submitted by a State Party which has made a declaration recognising in regard to itself the competence of the Committee. No communication shall be received by the Committee if it concerns a State Party which has not made such a declaration. Communications received under this article shall be dealt with in accordance with the following procedure:

(*a*) If a State Party to the present Covenant considers that another State Party is not giving effect to the provisions of the present Covenant, it may, by written communication, bring the matter to the attention of that State Party. Within three months after the receipt of the communication, the receiving State shall afford the State which sent the communication an explanation or any other statement in writing clarifying the matter, which should include, to the extent possible and pertinent, reference to domestic procedures and remedies taken, pending, or available in the matter.

(*b*) If the matter is not adjusted to the satisfaction of both States Parties concerned within six months after the receipt by the receiving State of the initial communication, either State shall have the right to refer the matter to the Committee, by notice given to the Committee and to the other State.

(*c*) The Committee shall deal with a matter referred to it only after it has ascertained that all available domestic remedies have been invoked and exhausted in the matter, in conformity with the generally recognised principles of international law. This shall not be the rule where the application of the remedies is unreasonably prolonged.

(*d*) The Committee shall hold closed meetings when examining communications under this article.

(*e*) Subject to the provisions of sub-paragraph (*c*), the Committee shall make available its good offices to the States Parties concerned with a view to a friendly solution of the matter on the basis of respect for human rights and fundamental freedoms as recognised in the present Covenant.

(*f*) In any matter referred to it, the Committee may call

upon the States Parties concerned, referred to in sub-paragraph (*b*), to supply any relevant information.

(*g*) The States Parties concerned, referred to in sub-paragraph (*b*), shall have the right to be represented when the matter is being considered in the Committee and to make submissions orally and/or in writing.

(*h*) The Committee shall, within twelve months after the date of receipt of notice under sub-paragraph (*b*), submit a report:

(i) If a solution within the terms of sub-paragraph (*e*) is reached, the Committee shall confine its report to a brief statement of the facts and of the solution reached;

(ii) If a solution within the terms of sub-paragraph (*e*) is not reached, the Committee shall confine its report to a brief statement of the facts; the written submissions and record of the oral submissions made by the States Parties concerned shall be attached to the report.

In every matter, the report shall be communicated to the States Parties concerned.

2. The provisions of this article shall come into force when ten States Parties to the present Covenant have made declarations under paragraph 1 of this article. Such declarations shall be deposited by the States Parties with the Secretary-General of the United Nations, who shall transmit copies thereof to the other States Parties. A declaration may be withdrawn at any time by notification to the Secretary-General. Such a withdrawal shall not prejudice the consideration of any matter which is the subject of a communication already transmitted under this article; no further communication by any State Party shall be received after the notification of withdrawal of the declaration has been received by the Secretary-General, unless the State Party concerned has made a new declaration.

Article 42

1. (*a*) If a matter referred to the Committee in accordance with article 41 is not resolved to the satisfaction of the States Parties concerned, the Committee may, with the prior consent of the States Parties concerned, appoint an *ad hoc* Conciliation Commission (hereinafter referred to as the Commission). The

good offices of the Commission shall be made available to the States Parties concerned with a view to an amicable solution of the matter on the basis of respect for the present Covenant;

(*b*) The Commission shall consist of five persons acceptable to the States Parties concerned. If the States Parties concerned fail to reach agreement within three months on all or part of the composition of the Commission, the members of the Commission concerning whom no agreement has been reached shall be elected by secret ballot by a two-thirds majority vote of the Committee from among its members.

2. The members of the Commission shall serve in their personal capacity. They shall not be nationals of the States Parties concerned, or of a State not party to the present Covenant, or of a State Party which has not made a declaration under article 41.

3. The Commission shall elect its own Chairman and adopt its own rules of procedure.

4. The meetings of the Commission shall normally be held at the Headquarters of the United Nations or at the United Nations Office at Geneva. However, they may be held at such other convenient places as the Commission may determine in consultation with the Secretary-General of the United Nations and the States Parties concerned.

5. The secretariat provided in accordance with article 36 shall also service the commissions appointed under this article.

6. The information received and collated by the Committee shall be made available to the Commission and the Commission may call upon the States Parties concerned to supply any other relevant information.

7. When the Commission has fully considered the matter, but in any event not later than twelve months after having been seized of the matter, it shall submit to the Chairman of the Committee a report for communication to the States Parties concerned:

(*a*) If the Commission is unable to complete its consideration of the matter within twelve months, it shall confine its report to a brief statement of the status of its consideration of the matter;

(*b*) If an amicable solution to the matter on the basis of respect for human rights as recognised in the present Covenant is reached, the Commission shall confine its report to a brief statement of the facts and of the solution reached;

(*c*) If a solution within the terms of sub-paragraph (*b*) is not reached, the Commission's report shall embody its findings on all questions of fact relevant to the issues between the States Parties concerned, and its views on the possibilities of an amicable solution of the matter. This report shall also contain the written submissions and a record of the oral submissions made by the States Parties concerned;

(*d*) If the Commission's report is submitted under sub-paragraph (*c*), the States Parties concerned shall, within three months of the receipt of the report, notify the Chairman of the Committee whether or not they accept the contents of the report of the Commission.

8. The provisions of this article are without prejudice to the responsibilities of the Committee under article 41.

9. The States Parties concerned shall share equally all the expenses of the members of the Commission in accordance with estimates to be provided by the Secretary-General of the United Nations.

10. The Secretary-General of the United Nations shall be empowered to pay the expenses of the members of the Commission, if necessary, before reimbursement by the States Parties concerned, in accordance with paragraph 9 of this article.

Article 43

The members of the Committee, and of the *ad hoc* conciliation commissions which may be appointed under article 42, shall be entitled to the facilities, privileges and immunities of experts on mission for the United Nations as laid down in the relevant sections of the Convention on the Privileges and Immunities of the United Nations.

Article 44

The provisions for the implementation of the present Covenant shall apply without prejudice to the procedures prescribed in the field of human rights by or under the constituent instruments and the conventions of the United Nations and of the specialised agencies and shall not prevent the States Parties to the present Covenant from having recourse to other procedures for settling a dispute in accordance with general or special international agreements in force between them.

Article 45

The Committee shall submit to the General Assembly of the United Nations, through the Economic and Social Council, an annual report on its activities.

PART V

Article 46

Nothing in the present Covenant shall be interpreted as impairing the provisions of the Charter of the United Nations and of the constitutions of the specialised agencies which define the respective responsibilities of the various organs of the United Nations and of the specialised agencies in regard to the matters dealt with in the present Covenant.

Article 47

Nothing in the present Covenant shall be interpreted as impairing the inherent right of all peoples to enjoy and utilise fully and freely their natural wealth and resources.

PART VI

Article 48

1. The present Covenant is open for signature by any State Member of the United Nations or member of any of its specialised agencies, by any State Party to the Statute of the International Court of Justice, and by any other State which has been invited by the General Assembly of the United Nations to become a party to the present Covenant.

2. The present Covenant is subject to ratification. Instruments of ratification shall be deposited with the Secretary-General of the United Nations.

3. The present Covenant shall be open to accession by any State referred to in paragraph 1 of this article.

4. Accession shall be effected by the deposit of an instrument of accession with the Secretary-General of the United Nations.

5. The Secretary-General of the United Nations shall inform all States which have signed this Covenant or acceded to it of the deposit of each instrument of ratification or accession.

Article 49

1. The present Covenant shall enter into force three months after the date of the deposit with the Secretary-General of the United Nations of the thirty-fifth instrument of ratification or instrument of accession.

2. For each State ratifying the present Covenant or acceding to it after the deposit of the thirty-fifth instrument of ratification or instrument of accession, the present Covenant shall enter into force three months after the date of the deposit of its own instrument of ratification or instrument of accession.

Article 50

The provisions of the present Covenant shall extend to all parts of federal States without any limitations or exceptions.

Article 51

1. Any State Party to the present Covenant may propose an amendment and file it with the Secretary-General of the United Nations. The Secretary-General of the United Nations shall thereupon communicate any proposed amendments to the States Parties to the present Covenant with a request that they notify him whether they favour a conference of States Parties for the purpose of considering and voting upon the proposals. In the event that at least one third of the States Parties favours such a conference, the Secretary-General shall convene the conference under the auspices of the United Nations. Any amendment adopted by a majority of the States Parties present and voting at the conference shall be submitted to the General Assembly of the United Nations for approval.

2. Amendments shall come into force when they have been approved by the General Assembly of the United Nations and

accepted by a two-thirds majority of the States Parties to the present Covenant in accordance with their respective constitutional processes.

3. When amendments come into force, they shall be binding on those States Parties which have accepted them, other States Parties still being bound by the provisions of the present Covenant and any earlier amendment which they have accepted.

Article 52

Irrespective of the notifications made under article 48, paragraph 5, the Secretary-General of the United Nations shall inform all States referred to in paragraph 1 of the same article of the following particulars:

(*a*) Signatures, ratifications and accessions under article 48;

(*b*) The date of the entry into force of the present Covenant under article 49 and the date of the entry into force of any amendments under article 51.

Article 53

1. The present Covenant, of which the Chinese, English, French, Russian and Spanish texts are equally authentic, shall be deposited in the archives of the United Nations.

2. The Secretary-General of the United Nations shall transmit certified copies of the present Covenant to all States referred to in article 48.

OPTIONAL PROTOCOL TO THE INTERNATIONAL COVENANT ON CIVIL AND POLITICAL RIGHTS

The States Parties to the present Protocol,

Considering that in order further to achieve the purposes of the Covenant on Civil and Political Rights (hereinafter referred to as the Covenant) and the implementation of its provisions it would be appropriate to enable the Human Rights Committee set up in part IV of the Covenant (hereinafter referred to as the Committee) to receive and consider, as provided in the present Protocol, communications from individuals claiming to be victims of violations of any of the rights set forth in the Covenant,

Have agreed as follows:

Article 1

A State Party to the Covenant that becomes a party to the present Protocol recognises the competence of the Committee to receive and consider communications from individuals subject to its jurisdiction who claim to be victims of a violation by that State Party of any of the rights set forth in the Covenant. No communication shall be received by the Committee if it concerns a State Party to the Covenant which is not a party to the present Protocol.

Article 2

Subject to the provisions of article 1, individuals who claim that any of their rights enumerated in the Covenant have been violated and who have exhausted all available domestic remedies may submit a written communication to the Committee for consideration.

Article 3

The Committee shall consider inadmissible any communication under the present Protocol which is anonymous, or which it considers to be an abuse of the right of submission of such communications or to be incompatible with the provisions of the Covenant.

Article 4

1. Subject to the provisions of article 3, the Committee shall bring any communications submitted to it under the present Protocol to the attention of the State Party to the present Protocol alleged to be violating any provision of the Covenant.

2. Within six months, the receiving State shall submit to the Committee written explanations or statements clarifying the matter and the remedy, if any, that may have been taken by that State.

Article 5

1. The Committee shall consider communications received under the present Protocol in the light of all written information made available to it by the individual and by the State Party concerned.

2. The Committee shall not consider any communication from an individual unless it has ascertained that:

(*a*) The same matter is not being examined under another procedure of international investigation or settlement;

(*b*) The individual has exhausted all available domestic remedies.

This shall not be the rule where the application of the remedies is unreasonably prolonged.

3. The Committee shall hold closed meetings when examining communications under the present Protocol.

4. The Committee shall forward its views to the State Party concerned and to the individual.

Article 6

The Committee shall include in its annual report under article 45 of the Covenant a summary of its activities under the present Protocol.

Article 7

Pending the achievement of the objectives of resolution 1514 (XV) adopted by the General Assembly of the United Nations on 14 December 1960 concerning the Declaration on the Granting of Independence to Colonial Countries and Peoples, the provisions of the present Protocol shall in no way limit the right of petition granted to these peoples by the Charter of the United Nations and other international conventions and instruments under the United Nations and its specialised agencies.

Article 8

1. The present Protocol is open for signature by any State which has signed the Covenant.

2. The present Protocol is subject to ratification by any

State which has ratified or acceded to the Covenant. Instruments of ratification shall be deposited with the Secretary-General of the United Nations.

3. The present Protocol shall be open to accession by any State which has ratified or acceded to the Covenant.

4. Accession shall be effected by the deposit of an instrument of accession with the Secretary-General of the United Nations.

5. The Secretary-General of the United Nations shall inform all States which have signed the present Protocol or acceded to it of the deposit of each instrument of ratification or accession.

Article 9

1. Subject to the entry into force of the Covenant, the present Protocol shall enter into force three months after the date of the deposit with the Secretary-General of the United Nations of the tenth instrument of ratification or instrument of accession.

2. For each State ratifying the present Protocol or acceding to it after the deposit of the tenth instrument of ratification or instrument of accession, the present Protocol shall enter into force three months after the date of the deposit of its own instrument of ratification or instrument of accession.

Article 10

The provisions of the present Protocol shall extend to all parts of federal States without any limitations or exceptions.

Article 11

1. Any State Party to the present Protocol may propose an amendment and file it with the Secretary-General of the United Nations. The Secretary-General shall thereupon communicate any proposed amendments to the States Parties to the present Protocol with a request that they notify him whether they favour a conference of States Parties for the purpose of considering and voting upon the proposal. In the event that at least one third of the States Parties favours such

133

a conference, the Secretary-General shall convene the conference under the auspices of the United Nations. Any amendment adopted by a majority of the States Parties present and voting at the conference shall be submitted to the General Assembly of the United Nations for approval.

2. Amendments shall come into force when they have been approved by the General Assembly of the United Nations and accepted by a two-thirds majority of the States Parties to the present Protocol in accordance with their respective constitutional processes.

3. When amendments come into force, they shall be binding on those States Parties which have accepted them, other States Parties still being bound by the provisions of the present Protocol and any earlier amendment which they have accepted.

Article 12

1. Any State Party may denounce the present Protocol at any time by written notification addressed to the Secretary-General of the United Nations. Denunciation shall take effect three months after the date of receipt of the notification by the Secretary-General.

2. Denunciation shall be without prejudice to the continued application of the provisions of the present Protocol to any communication submitted under article 2 before the effective date of denunciation.

Article 13

Irrespective of the notifications made under article 8, paragraph 5, of the present Protocol, the Secretary-General of the United Nations shall inform all States referred to in article 48, paragraph 1, of the Covenant of the following particulars:

(*a*) Signatures, ratifications and accessions under article 8;

(*b*) The date of the entry into force of the present Protocol under article 9 and the date of the entry into force of any amendments under article 11;

(*c*) Denunciations under article 12.

Article 14

1. The present Protocol, of which the Chinese, English, French, Russian and Spanish texts are equally authentic, shall be deposited in the archives of the United Nations.

2. The Secretary-General of the United Nations shall transmit certified copies of the present Protocol to all States referred to in article 48 of the Covenant.

Appendix C

EUROPEAN CONVENTION FOR THE PROTECTION OF HUMAN RIGHTS AND FUNDAMENTAL FREEDOMS

The Governments signatory hereto, being Members of the Council of Europe,

Considering the Universal Declaration of Human Rights proclaimed by the General Assembly of the United Nations on 10th December 1948;

Considering that this Declaration aims at securing the universal and effective recognition and observance of the Rights therein declared;

Considering that the aim of the Council of Europe is the achievement of greater unity between its Members and that one of the methods by which that aim is to be pursued is the maintenance and further realisation of Human Rights and Fundamental Freedoms;

Reaffirming their profound belief in those Fundamental Freedoms which are the foundation of justice and peace in the world and are best maintained on the one hand by an effective political democracy and on the other by a common understanding and observance of the Human Rights upon which they depend;

Being resolved, as the Governments of European countries which are like-minded and have a common heritage of political traditions, ideals, freedom and the rule of law, to take the first steps for the collective enforcement of certain of the Rights stated in the Universal Declaration;

Have agreed as follows:

Article 1

The High Contracting Parties shall secure to everyone within their jurisdiction the rights and freedoms defined in Section I of this Convention.

SECTION I

Article 2

1. Everyone's right to life shall be protected by law. No one shall be deprived of his life intentionally save in the execution of a sentence of a court following his conviction of a crime for which this penalty is provided by law.

2. Deprivation of life shall not be regarded as inflicted in contravention of this Article when it results from the use of force which is no more than absolutely necessary:

(*a*) in defence of any person from unlawful violence;

(*b*) in order to effect a lawful arrest or to prevent the escape of a person lawfully detained;

(*c*) in action lawfully taken for the purpose of quelling a riot or insurrection.

Article 3

No one shall be subjected to torture or to inhuman or degrading treatment or punishment.

Article 4

1. No one shall be held in slavery or servitude.

2. No one shall be required to perform forced or compulsory labour.

3. For the purpose of this Article the term 'forced or compulsory labour' shall not include:

(*a*) any work required to be done in the ordinary course of detention imposed according to the provisions of Article 5 of this Convention or during conditional release from such detention;

(*b*) any service of a military character or, in case of conscientious objectors in countries where they are recognised, service exacted instead of compulsory military service;

(*c*) any service exacted in case of an emergency or calamity threatening the life or well-being of the community;

(*d*) any work or service which forms part of normal civic obligations.

Article 5

1. Everyone has the right to liberty and security of person. No one shall be deprived of his liberty save in the following cases and in accordance with a procedure prescribed by law:

(*a*) the lawful detention of a person after conviction by a competent court;

(*b*) the lawful arrest or detention of a person for non-compliance with the lawful order of a court or in order to secure the fulfilment of any obligation prescribed by law;

(*c*) the lawful arrest or detention of a person effected for the purpose of bringing him before the competent legal authority on reasonable suspicion of having committed an offence or when it is reasonably considered necessary to prevent his committing an offence or fleeing after having done so;

(*d*) the detention of a minor by lawful order for the purpose of educational supervision or his lawful detention for the purpose of bringing him before the competent legal authority;

(*e*) the lawful detention of persons for the prevention of the spreading of infectious diseases, of persons of unsound mind, alcoholics or drug addicts or vagrants;

(*f*) the lawful arrest or detention of a person to prevent his effecting an unauthorised entry into the country or of a person against whom action is being taken with a view to deportation or extradition.

2. Everyone who is arrested shall be informed promptly, in a language which he understands, of the reasons for his arrest and of any charge against him.

3. Everyone arrested or detained in accordance with the provisions of paragraph 1 (*c*) of this Article shall be brought promptly before a judge or other officer authorised by law to exercise judicial power and shall be entitled to trial within a reasonable time or to release pending trial. Release may be conditioned by guarantees to appear for trial.

4. Everyone who is deprived of his liberty by arrest or detention shall be entitled to take proceedings by which the lawfulness of his detention shall be decided speedily by a court and his release ordered if the detention is not lawful.

5. Everyone who has been the victim of arrest or detention in

contravention of the provisions of this Article shall have an enforceable right of compensation.

Article 6

1. In the determination of his civil rights and obligations or of any criminal charge against him, everyone is entitled to a fair and public hearing within a reasonable time by an independent and impartial tribunal established by law. Judgement shall be pronounced publicly but the press and public may be excluded from all or part of the trial in the interest of morals, public order or national security in a democratic society, where the interests of juveniles or the protection of the private life of the parties so require, or to the extent strictly necessary in the opinion of the court in special circumstances where publicity would prejudice the interests of justice.

2. Everyone charged with a criminal offence shall be presumed innocent until proved guilty according to law.

3. Everyone charged with a criminal offence has the following minimum rights:

(*a*) to be informed promptly, in a language which he understands and in detail, of the nature and cause of the accusation against him;

(*b*) to have adequate time and facilities for the preparation of his defence;

(*c*) to defend himself in person or through legal assistance of his own choosing or, if he has not sufficient means to pay for legal assistance, to be given it free when the interests of justice so require;

(*d*) to examine or have examined witnesses against him and to obtain the attendance and examination of witnesses on his behalf under the same conditions as witnesses against him;

(*e*) to have the free assistance of an interpreter if he cannot understand or speak the language used in court.

Article 7

1. No one shall be held guilty of any criminal offence on account of any act or omission which did not constitute a criminal offence under national or international law at the time when it was committed. Nor shall a heavier penalty be imposed

than the one that was applicable at the time the criminal offence was committed.

2. This Article shall not prejudice the trial and punishment of any person for any act or omission which, at the time when it was committed, was criminal according to the general principles of law recognised by civilised nations.

Article 8

1. Everyone has the right to respect for his private and family life, his home and his correspondence.

2. There shall be no interference by a public authority with the exercise of this right except such as is in accordance with the law and is necessary in a democratic society in the interests of national security, public safety or the economic well-being of the country, for the prevention of disorder or crime, for the protection of health or morals, or for the protection of the rights and freedoms of others.

Article 9

1. Everyone has the right to freedom of thought, conscience and religion; this right includes freedom to change his religion or belief and freedom, either alone or in community with others and in public or private, to manifest his religion or belief, in worship, teaching, practice and observance.

2. Freedom to manifest one's religion or beliefs shall be subject only to such limitations as are prescribed by law and are necessary in a democratic society in the interests of public safety, for the protection of public order, health or morals, or for the protection of the rights and freedoms of others.

Article 10

1. Everyone has the right to freedom of expression. This right shall include freedom to hold opinions and to receive and impart information and ideas without interference by public authority and regardless of frontiers. This Article shall not prevent States from requiring the licensing of broadcasting, television or cinema enterprises.

2. The exercise of these freedoms, since it carries with it duties and responsibilities, may be subject to such formalities,

conditions, restrictions or penalties as are prescribed by law and are necessary in a democratic society, in the interests of national security, territorial integrity or public safety, for the prevention of disorder or crime, for the protection of health or morals, for the protection of the reputation or rights of others, for preventing the disclosure of information received in confidence, or for maintaining the authority and impartiality of the judiciary.

Article 11

1. Everyone has the right to freedom of peaceful assembly and to freedom of association with others, including the right to form and to join trade unions for the protection of his interests.

2. No restrictions shall be placed on the exercise of these rights other than such as are prescribed by law and are necessary in a democratic society in the interests of national security or public safety, for the prevention of disorder or crime, for the protection of health or morals or for the protection of the rights and freedoms of others. This Article shall not prevent the imposition of lawful restrictions on the exercise of these rights by members of the armed forces, of the police or of the administration of the State.

Article 12

Men and women of marriageable age have the right to marry and to found a family, according to the national laws governing the exercise of this right.

Article 13

Everyone whose rights and freedoms as set forth in this Convention are violated shall have an effective remedy before a national authority notwithstanding that the violation has been committed by persons acting in an official capacity.

Article 14

The enjoyment of the rights and freedoms set forth in this Convention shall be secured without discrimination on any ground such as sex, race, colour, language, religion, political or other opinion, national or social origin, association with a national minority, property, birth or other status.

Article 15

1. In time of war or other public emergency threatening the life of the nation any High Contracting Party may take measures derogating from its obligations under this Convention to the extent strictly required by the exigencies of the situation, provided that such measures are not inconsistent with its other obligations under international law.

2. No derogation from Article 2, except in respect of deaths resulting from lawful acts of war, or from Articles 3, 4 (paragraph 1) and 7 shall be made under this provision.

3. Any High Contracting Party availing itself of this right of derogation shall keep the Secretary-General of the Council of Europe fully informed of the measures which it has taken and the reasons therefore. It shall also inform the Secretary-General of the Council of Europe when such measures have ceased to operate and the provisions of the Convention are again being fully executed.

Article 16

Nothing in Articles 10, 11 and 14 shall be regarded as preventing the High Contracting Parties from imposing restrictions on the political activity of aliens.

Article 17

Nothing in this Convention may be interpreted as implying for any State, group or person any right to engage in any activity or perform any act aimed at the destruction of any of the rights and freedoms set forth herein or at their limitation to a greater extent than is provided for in the Convention.

Article 18

The restrictions permitted under this Convention to the said rights and freedoms shall not be applied for any purpose other than those for which they have been prescribed.

SECTION II

Article 19

To ensure the observance of the engagements undertaken by the High Contracting Parties in the present Convention, there shall be set up:

1. A European Commission of Human Rights hereinafter referred to as 'the Commission'.

2. A European Court of Human Rights, hereinafter referred to as 'the Court'.

SECTION III

Article 20

The Commission shall consist of a number of members equal to that of the High Contracting Parties. No two members of the Commission may be nationals of the same State.

Article 21

1. The members of the Commission shall be elected by the Committee of Ministers by an absolute majority of votes, from a list of names drawn up by the Bureau of the Consultative Assembly; each group of the Representatives of the High Contracting Parties in the Consultative Assembly shall put forward three candidates, of whom two at least shall be its nationals.

2. As far as applicable, the same procedure shall be followed to complete the Commission in the event of other States subsequently becoming Parties to this Convention, and in filling casual vacancies.

Article 22

1. The members of the Commission shall be elected for a period of six years. They may be re-elected. However, of the members elected at the first election, the terms of seven members shall expire at the end of three years.

2. The members whose terms are to expire at the end of the initial period of three years shall be chosen by lot by the

Secretary-General of the Council of Europe immediately after the first election has been completed.

3. A member of the Commission elected to replace a member whose term of office has not expired shall hold office for the remainder of his predecessor's term.

4. The members of the Commission shall hold office until replaced. After having been replaced, they shall continue to deal with such cases as they already have under consideration.

Article 23

The members of the Commission shall sit on the Commission in their individual capacity.

Article 24

Any High Contracting Party may refer to the Commission, through the Secretary-General of the Council of Europe, any alleged breach of the provisions of the Convention by another High Contracting Party.

Article 25

1. The Commission may receive petitions addressed to the Secretary-General of the Council of Europe from any person, non-governmental organisation or group of individuals claiming to be the victim of a violation by one of the High Contracting Parties of the rights set forth in this Convention, provided that the High Contracting Party against which the complaint has been lodged has declared that it recognises the competence of the Commission to receive such petitions. Those of the High Contracting Parties who have made such a declaration undertake not to hinder in any way the effective exercise of this right.

2. Such declarations may be made for a specific period.

3. The declarations shall be deposited with the Secretary-General of the Council of Europe who shall transmit copies thereof to the High Contracting Parties and publish them.

4. The Commission shall only exercise the powers provided for in this Article when at least six High Contracting Parties are bound by declarations made in accordance with the preceding paragraphs.

Article 26

The Commission may only deal with the matter after all domestic remedies have been exhausted, according to the generally recognised rules of international law, and within a period of six months from the date on which the final decision was taken.

Article 27

(1) The Commission shall not deal with any petition submitted under Article 25 which

(a) is anonymous, or

(b) is substantially the same as a matter which has already been examined by the Commission or has already been submitted to another procedure of international investigation or settlement and if it contains no relevant new information.

(2) The Commission shall consider inadmissible any petition submitted under Article 25 which it considers incompatible with the provisions of the present Convention, manifestly ill-founded, or an abuse of the right of petition.

(3) The Commission shall reject any petition referred to it which it considers inadmissible under Article 26.

Article 28

In the event of the Commission accepting a petition referred to it:

(a) it shall, with a view to ascertaining the facts, undertake together with the representatives of the parties an examination of the petition and, if need be, an investigation, for the effective conduct of which the States concerned shall furnish all necessary facilities, after an exchange of views with the Commission;

(b) it shall place itself at the disposal of the parties concerned with a view to securing a friendly settlement of the matter on the basis of respect for Human Rights as defined in this Convention.

Article 29[1]

After it has accepted a petition submitted under Article 25, the Commission may nevertheless decide unanimously to reject the petition if, in the course of its examination, it finds that the existence of one of the grounds for non-acceptance provided for in Article 27 has been established.

In such a case, the decision shall be communicated to the parties.

Article 30[2]

If the Commission succeeds in effecting a friendly settlement in accordance with Article 28, it shall draw up a Report which shall be sent to the States concerned, to the Committee of Ministers and to the Secretary-General of the Council of Europe for publication. This Report shall be confined to a brief statement of the facts and of the solution reached.

Article 31

(1) If a solution is not reached, the Commission shall draw up a Report on the facts and state its opinion as to whether the facts found disclose a breach by the State concerned of its obligations under the Convention. The opinions of all the members of the Commission on this point may be stated in the Report.

(2) The Report shall be transmitted to the Committee of Ministers. It shall also be transmitted to the States concerned, who shall not be at liberty to publish it.

(3) In transmitting the Report to the Committee of Ministers the Commission may make such proposals as it thinks fit.

Article 32

(1) If the question is not referred to the Court in accordance with Article 48 of this Convention within a period of three months from the date of the transmission of the Report to the Committee of Ministers, the Committee of Ministers shall decide by a majority of two-thirds of the members entitled to sit on the Committee whether there has been a violation of the Convention.

(2) In the affirmative case the Committee of Ministers shall prescribe a period during which the High Contracting Party concerned must take the measures required by the decision of the Committee of Ministers.

(3) If the High Contracting Party concerned has not taken

satisfactory measures within the prescribed period, the Committee of Ministers shall decide by the majority provided for in paragraph (1) above what effect shall be given to its original decision and shall publish the Report.

(4) The High Contracting Parties undertake to regard as binding on them any decision which the Committee of Ministers may take in application of the preceding paragraphs.

Article 33

The Commission shall meet in camera.

Article 34[3]

Subject to the provisions of Article 29, the Commission shall take its decisions by a majority of the Members present and voting.

Article 35

The Commission shall meet as the circumstances require. The meetings shall be convened by the Secretary-General of the Council of Europe.

Article 36

The Commission shall draw up its own rules of procedure.

Article 37

The secretariat of the Commission shall be provided by the Secretary-General of the Council of Europe.

SECTION IV

Article 38

The European Court of Human Rights shall consist of a number of judges equal to that of the Members of the Council of Europe. No two judges may be nationals of the same State.

Article 39

1. The members of the Court shall be elected by the Consultative Assembly by a majority of the votes cast from a list of

persons nominated by the Members of the Council of Europe; each Member shall nominate three candidates, of whom two at least shall be its nationals.

2. As far as applicable, the same procedure shall be followed to complete the Court in the event of the admission of new Members of the Council of Europe, and in filling casual vacancies.

3. The candidates shall be of high moral character and must either possess the qualifications required for appointment to high judicial office or be jurisconsults of recognised competence.

Article 40

1. The members of the Court shall be elected for a period of nine years. They may be re-elected. However, of the members elected at the first election the terms of four members shall expire at the end of three years, and the terms of four more members shall expire at the end of six years.

2. The members whose terms are to expire at the end of the initial periods of three and six years shall be chosen by lot by the Secretary-General immediately after the first election has been completed.

3. A member of the Court elected to replace a member whose term of office has not expired shall hold office for the remainder of his predecessor's term.

4. The members of the Court shall hold office until replaced. After having been replaced, they shall continue to deal with such cases as they already have under consideration.

Article 41

The Court shall elect its President and Vice-President for a period of three years. They may be re-elected.

Article 42

The members of the Court shall receive for each day of duty a compensation to be determined by the Committee of Ministers.

Article 43

For the consideration of each case brought before it the Court shall consist of a Chamber composed of seven judges. There shall sit as an ex officio member of the Chamber the judge who is a national of any State party concerned, or, if there is none, a person of its choice who shall sit in the capacity of judge; the names of the other judges shall be chosen by lot by the President before the opening of the case.

Article 44

Only the High Contracting Parties and the Commission shall have the right to bring a case before the Court.

Article 45

The jurisdiction of the Court shall extend to all cases concerning the interpretation and application of the present Convention which the High Contracting Parties or the Commission shall refer to it in accordance with Article 48.

Article 46

1. Any of the High Contracting Parties may at any time declare that it recognises as compulsory *ipso facto* and without special agreement the jurisdiction of the Court in all matters concerning the interpretation and application of the present Convention.

2. The declarations referred to above may be made unconditionally or on condition of reciprocity on the part of several or certain other High Contracting Parties or for a specified period.

3. These declarations shall be deposited with the Secretary-General of the Council of Europe who shall transmit copies thereof to the High Contracting Parties.

Article 47

The Court may only deal with a case after the Commission has acknowledged the failure of efforts for a friendly settlement and within the period of three months provided for in Article 32.

Article 48

The following may bring a case before the Court, provided that the High Contracting Party concerned, if there is only one, or the High Contracting Parties concerned, if there is more than one, are subject to the compulsory jurisdiction of the Court or, failing that, with the consent of the High Contracting Party concerned, if there is only one, or of the High Contracting Parties concerned if there is more than one:

(*a*) the Commission;

(*b*) a High Contracting Party whose national is alleged to be a victim;

(*c*) a High Contracting Party which referred the case to the Commission;

(*d*) a High Contracting Party against which the complaint has been lodged.

Article 49

In the event of dispute as to whether the Court has jurisdiction, the matter shall be settled by the decision of the Court.

Article 50

If the Court finds that a decision or a measure taken by a legal authority or any other authority of a High Contracting Party is completely or partially in conflict with the obligations arising from the present Convention, and if the internal law of the said Party allows only partial reparation to be made for the consequences of this decision or measure, the decision of the Court shall, if necessary, afford just satisfaction to the injured party.

Article 51

1. Reasons shall be given for the judgement of the Court.

2. If the judgement does not represent in whole or in part the unanimous opinion of the judges, any judge shall be entitled to deliver a separate opinion.

Article 52

The judgement of the Court shall be final.

Article 53

The High Contracting Parties undertake to abide by the decision of the Court in any case to which they are parties.

Article 54

The judgement of the Court shall be transmitted to the Committee of Ministers which shall supervise its execution.

Article 55

The Court shall draw up its own rules and shall determine its own procedure.

Article 56

1. The first election of the members of the Court shall take place after the declarations by the High Contracting Parties mentioned in Article 46 have reached a total of eight.

2. No case can be brought before the Court before this election.

SECTION V

Article 57

On receipt of a request from the Secretary-General of the Council of Europe any High Contracting Party shall furnish an explanation of the manner in which its internal law ensures the effective implementation of any of the provisions of this Convention.

Article 58

The expenses of the Commission and the Court shall be borne by the Council of Europe.

Article 59

The members of the Commission and of the Court shall be entitled, during the discharge of their functions, to the privileges and immunities provided for in Article 40 of the Statute of the Council of Europe and in the agreements made thereunder.

Article 60

Nothing in this Convention shall be construed as limiting or derogating from any of the human rights and fundamental freedoms which may be ensured under the laws of any High

Contracting Party or under any other agreement to which it is a Party.

Article 61

Nothing in this Convention shall prejudice the powers conferred on the Committee of Ministers by Statute of the Council of Europe.

Article 62

The High Contracting Parties agree that, except by special agreement, they will not avail themselves of treaties, conventions or declarations in force between them for the purpose of submitting, by way of petition, a dispute arising out of the interpretation or application of this Convention to a means of settlement other than those provided for in this Convention.

Article 63

1. Any State may at the time of its ratification or at any time thereafter declare by notification addressed to the Secretary-General of the Council of Europe that the present Convention shall extend to all or any of the territories for whose international relations it is responsible.

2. The Convention shall extend to the territory or territories named in the notification as from the thirtieth day after the receipt of this notification by the Secretary-General of the Council of Europe.

3. The provisions of this Convention shall be applied in such territories with due regard, however, to local requirements.

4. Any State which has made a declaration in accordance with paragraph 1 of this Article may at any time thereafter declare on behalf of one or more of the territories to which the declaration relates that it accepts the competence of the Commission to receive petitions from individuals, non-governmental organisations or groups of individuals in accordance with Article 25 of the present Convention.

Article 64

1. Any State may, when signing this Convention or when depositing its instrument of ratification, make a reservation in

respect of any particular provision of the Convention to the extent that any law then in force in its territory is not in conformity with the provision. Reservations of a general character shall not be permitted under this Article.

2. Any reservation made under this Article shall contain a brief statement of the law concerned.

Article 65

1. A High Contracting Party may denounce the present Convention only after the expiry of five years from the date on which it became a Party to it and after six months' notice contained in a notification addressed to the Secretary-General of the Council of Europe, who shall inform the other High Contracting Parties.

2. Such a denunciation shall not have the effect of releasing the High Contracting Party concerned from its obligations under this Convention in respect of any act which, being capable of constituting a violation of such obligations, may have been performed by it before the date at which the denunciation became effective.

3. Any High Contracting Party which shall cease to be a Member of the Council of Europe shall cease to be a Party to this Convention under the same conditions.

4. The Convention may be denounced in accordance with the provisions of the preceding paragraphs in respect of any territory to which it has been declared to extend under the terms of Article 63.

Article 66

1. This Convention shall be open to the signature of the Members of the Council of Europe. It shall be ratified. Ratifications shall be deposited with the Secretary-General of the Council of Europe.

2. The present Convention shall come into force after the deposit of ten instruments of ratification.

3. As regards any signatory ratifying subsequently, the Convention shall come into force at the date of the deposit of its instrument of ratification.

4. The Secretary-General of the Council of Europe shall

notify all the Members of the Council of Europe of the entry into force of the Convention, the names of the High Contracting Parties who have ratified it, and the deposit of all instruments of ratification which may be effected subsequently.

DONE at Rome this 4th day of November 1950 in English and French, both texts being equally authentic, in a single copy which shall remain deposited in the archives of the Council of Europe. The Secretary-General shall transmit certified copies to each of the signatories.

(Signed on behalf of the governments of Austria, Belgium, Cyprus, Denmark, France, West Germany, Greece, Iceland, Ireland, Italy, Luxembourg, Malta, Netherlands, Norway, Sweden, Turkey, and the United Kingdom.)

PROTOCOL TO THE CONVENTION FOR THE PROTECTION OF HUMAN RIGHTS AND FUNDAMENTAL FREEDOMS

The Governments signatory hereto, being Members of the Council of Europe,

Being resolved to take steps to ensure the collective enforcement of certain rights and freedoms other than those already included in Section I of the Convention for the Protection of Human Rights and Fundamental Freedoms signed at Rome on 4th November 1950 (hereinafter referred to as 'the Convention'),

Have agreed as follows:

Article 1

Every natural or legal person is entitled to the peaceful enjoyment of his possessions. No one shall be deprived of his possessions except in the public interest and subject to the conditions provided for by law and by the general principles of international law.

The preceding provisions shall not, however, in any way impair the right of a State to enforce such laws as it deems necessary to control the use of property in accordance with the general interest or to secure the payment of taxes or other contributions or penalties.

Article 2

No person shall be denied the right to education. In the exercise of any functions which it assumes in relation to education and to teaching, the State shall respect the right of parents to ensure such education and teaching in conformity with their own religious and philosophical convictions.

Article 3

The High Contracting Parties undertake to hold free elections at reasonable intervals by secret ballot, under conditions which will ensure the free expression of the opinion of the people in the choice of the legislature.

Article 4

Any High Contracting Party may at the time of signature or ratification or at any time thereafter communicate to the Secretary-General of the Council of Europe a declaration stating the extent to which it undertakes that the provisions of the present Protocol shall apply to such of the territories for the international relations of which it is responsible as are named therein.

Any High Contracting Party which has communicated a declaration in virtue of the preceding paragraph may from time to time communicate a further declaration modifying the terms of any former declaration or terminating the application of the provisions of this Protocol in respect of any territory.

A declaration made in accordance with this Article shall be deemed to have been made in accordance with paragraph (1) of Article 63 of the Convention.

Article 5

As between the High Contracting Parties the provisions of Articles 1, 2, 3, and 4 of this Protocol shall be regarded as additional Articles to the Convention and all the provisions of the Convention shall apply accordingly.

Article 6

This Protocol shall be open for signature by the Members of the Council of Europe, who are the signatories of the Convention; it shall be ratified at the same time as or after the ratification of the Convention. It shall enter into force after the deposit of ten instruments of ratification. As regards any signatory ratifying subsequently, the Protocol shall enter into force at the date of the deposit of its instrument of ratification.

The instruments of ratification shall be deposited with the Secretary-General of the Council of Europe, who will notify all Members of the names of those who have ratified.

DONE at Paris on the 20th day of March 1952, in English and French, both texts being equally authentic, in a single copy which shall remain deposited in the archives of the Council of Europe. The Secretary-General shall transmit certified copies to each of the signatory Governments.

(Signed on behalf of the Governments of Austria, Belgium, Cyprus, Denmark, France, German Federal Republic, Greece, the Irish Republic, Italy, Luxembourg, Malta, Netherlands, Norway, Sweden, Turkey, and the United Kingdom.)

PROTOCOL No. 2 TO THE CONVENTION FOR THE PROTECTION OF HUMAN RIGHTS AND FUNDA-MENTAL FREEDOMS,
conferring upon the European Court of Human Rights competence to give advisory opinions

The member States of the Council of Europe signatory hereto:

Having regard to the provisions of the Convention for the Protection of Human Rights and Fundamental Freedoms signed at Rome on 4th November 1950 (hereinafter referred to as 'the Convention') and, in particular, Article 19 instituting, among other bodies, a European Court of Human Rights (hereinafter referred to as 'the Court');

Considering that it is expedient to confer upon the Court

competence to give advisory opinions subject to certain conditions:

Have agreed as follows:

Article 1

1. The Court may, at the request of the Committee of Ministers, give advisory opinions on legal questions concerning the interpretation of the Convention and the Protocols thereto.

2. Such opinions shall not deal with any question relating to the content or scope of the rights or freedoms defined in Section 1 of the Convention and in the Protocols thereto, or with any other question which the Commission, the Court or the Committee of Ministers might have to consider in consequence of any such proceedings as could be instituted in accordance with the Convention.

3. Decisions of the Committee of Ministers to request an advisory opinion of the Court shall require a two-thirds majority vote of the representatives entitled to sit on the Committee.

Article 2

The Court shall decide whether a request for an advisory opinion submitted by the Committee of Ministers is within its consultative competence as defined in Article 1 of this Protocol.

Article 3

1. For the consideration of requests for an advisory opinion, the Court shall sit in plenary session.

2. Reasons shall be given for advisory opinions of the Court.

3. If the advisory opinion does not represent in whole or in part the unanimous opinion of the judges, any judge shall be entitled to deliver a separate opinion.

4. Advisory opinions of the Court shall be communicated to the Committee of Ministers.

Article 4

The powers of the Court under Article 55 of the Convention shall extend to the drawing up of such rules and the determination of such procedure as the Court may think necessary for the purposes of this Protocol.

Article 5

1. This Protocol shall be open to signature by member States of the Council of Europe, signatories to the Convention, who may become Parties to it by:

(*a*) signature without reservation in respect of ratification or acceptance;

(*b*) signature with reservation in respect of ratification or acceptance, followed by ratification or acceptance.

Instruments of ratification or acceptance shall be deposited with the Secretary-General of the Council of Europe.

2. This Protocol shall enter into force as soon as all States Parties to the Convention shall have become Parties to the Protocol, in accordance with the provisions of paragraph 1 of this Article.

3. From the date of the entry into force of this Protocol, Articles 1 to 4 shall be considered an integral part of the Convention.

4. The Secretary-General of the Council of Europe shall notify the member States of the Council of:

(*a*) any signature without reservation in respect of ratification or acceptance;

(*b*) any signature with reservation in respect of ratification or acceptance;

(*c*) the deposit of any instrument of ratification or acceptance;

(*d*) the date of entry into force of this Protocol in accordance with paragraph 2 of this Article.

In witness whereof, the undersigned, being duly authorised thereto, have signed this Protocol.

Done at Strasbourg, this 6th day of May 1963, in English and in French, both texts being equally authoritative, in a single copy which shall remain deposited in the archives of the Council of Europe. The Secretary-General shall transmit certified copies to each of the signatory States.

(Signed on behalf of the Governments of Austria, Belgium,

Cyprus, Denmark, West Germany, Iceland, Ireland, Italy, Luxembourg, Malta, Netherlands, Norway, Sweden, Turkey, and the United Kingdom.)

PROTOCOL No. 3 TO THE CONVENTION FOR THE PROTECTION OF HUMAN RIGHTS AND FUNDAMENTAL FREEDOMS,

amending Articles 29, 30 and 34 of the Convention

The member States of the Council of Europe, signatories to this Protocol,

Considering that it is advisable to amend certain provisions of the Convention for the Protection of Human Rights and Fundamental Freedoms signed at Rome on 4th November 1950 (hereinafter referred to as 'the Convention') concerning the procedure of the European Commission of Human Rights,

Have agreed as follows:

Article 1

1. Article 29 of the Convention is deleted.

2. The following provision shall be inserted in the Convention:

'Article 29. After it has accepted a petition submitted under Article 25, the Commission may nevertheless decide unanimously to reject the petition if, in the course of its examination, it finds that the existence of one of the grounds for non-acceptance provided for in Article 27 has been established.

In such a case, the decision shall be communicated to the parties.'

Article 2

In Article 30 of the Convention, the word 'Sub-Commission' shall be replaced by the word "Commission'.

Article 3

1. At the beginning of Article 34 of the Convention, the following shall be inserted:

'Subject to the provisions of Article 29 . . .'

2. At the end of the same Article, the sentence 'the Sub-Commission shall take its decisions by a majority of its members' shall be deleted.

Article 4

1. This Protocol shall be open to signature by the member States of the Council of Europe signatories to the Convention,[4] who may become Parties to it either by:

(a) signature without reservation in respect of ratification or acceptance, or

(b) signature with reservation in respect of ratification or acceptance, followed by ratification or acceptance.

Instruments of ratification or acceptance shall be deposited with the Secretary-General of the Council of Europe.

2. This Protocol shall enter into force as soon as all States Parties to the Convention shall have become Parties to the Protocol, in accordance with the provisions of paragraph 1 of this Article.

3. The Secretary-General of the Council of Europe shall notify the member States of the Council of:

(a) any signature without reservation in respect of ratification or acceptance;

(b) any signature with reservation in respect of ratification or acceptance;

(c) the deposit of any instrument of ratification or acceptance;

(d) the date of entry into force of this Protocol in accordance with paragraph 2 of this Article.

In witness whereof, the undersigned being duly authorised thereto, have signed this Protocol.

Done at Strasbourg, this 6th day of May 1963, in English and in French, both texts being equally authoritative, in a single copy which shall remain deposited in the archives of the Council of Europe. The Secretary-General shall transmit certified copies to each of the signatory States.

(Signed on behalf of the Governments of Austria, Belgium, Cyprus, Denmark, West Germany, Greece,[5] Iceland, Ireland,

Italy, Luxembourg, Netherlands, Norway, Sweden, Turkey, the United Kingdom, and Malta.)

PROTOCOL No. 4 TO THE CONVENTION FOR THE PROTECTION OF HUMAN RIGHTS AND FUNDAMENTAL FREEDOMS,

securing certain rights and freedoms other than those already included in the Convention and in the first Protocol thereto

The Governments signatory hereto, being Members of the Council of Europe,

Being resolved to take steps to ensure the collective enforcement of certain rights and freedoms other than those already included in Section I of the Convention for the Protection of Human Rights and Fundamental Freedoms signed at Rome on 4th November 1950 (hereinafter referred to as 'the Convention') and in Articles 1 to 3 of the First Protocol to the Convention, signed at Paris on 20th March 1952,

Have agreed as follows:

Article 1

No one shall be deprived of his liberty merely on the ground of inability to fulfil a contractual obligation.

Article 2

1. Everyone lawfully within the territory of a State shall, within that territory, have the right to liberty of movement and freedom to choose his residence.

2. Everyone shall be free to leave any country, including his own.

3. No restrictions shall be placed on the exercise of these rights other than such as are in accordance with law and are necessary in a democratic society in the interests of national security or public safety, for the maintenance of *ordre public*, for the prevention of crime, for the protection of health or morals, or for the protection of the rights and freedoms of others.

4. The rights set forth in paragraph 1 may also be subject, in

particular areas, to restrictions imposed in accordance with law and justified by the public interest in a democratic society.

Article 3

1. No one shall be expelled, by means either of an individual or of a collective measure, from the territory of the State of which he is a national.

2. No one shall be deprived of the right to enter the territory of the State of which he is a national.

Article 4

Collective expulsion of aliens is prohibited.

Article 5

1. Any High Contracting Party may, at the time of signature or ratification of this Protocol, or at any time thereafter, communicate to the Secretary-General of the Council of Europe a declaration stating the extent to which it undertakes that the provisions of this Protocol shall apply to such of the territories for the international relations of which it is responsible as are named therein.

2. Any High Contracting Party which has communicated a declaration in virtue of the preceding paragraph may, from time to time, communicate a further declaration modifying the terms of any former declaration or terminating the application of the provisions of this Protocol in respect of any territory.

3. A declaration made in accordance with this article shall be deemed to have been made in accordance with paragraph 1 of Article 63 of the Convention.

4. The territory of any State to which this Protocol applies by virtue of ratification or acceptance by that State, and each territory to which this Protocol is applied by virtue of a declaration by that State under this Article, shall be treated as separate territories for the purpose of the references in Articles 2 and 3 to the territory of a State.

Article 6

1. As between the High Contracting Parties the provisions of Articles 1 to 5 of this Protocol shall be regarded as additional

Articles to the Convention, and all the provisions of the Convention shall apply accordingly.

2. Nevertheless, the right of individual recourse recognised by a declaration made under Article 25 of the Convention, or the acceptance of the compulsory jurisdiction of the Court by a declaration made under Article 46 of the Convention, shall not be effective in relation to this Protocol unless the High Contracting Party concerned has made a statement recognising such right, or accepting such jurisdiction, in respect of all or any of Articles 1 to 4 of the Protocol.

Article 7

1. This Protocol shall be open for signature by the Members of the Council of Europe who are the signatories of the Convention; it shall be ratified at the same time as or after the ratification of the Convention. It shall enter into force after the deposit of five instruments of ratification. As regards any signatory ratifying subsequently, the Protocol shall enter into force at the date of the deposit of its instrument of ratification.

2. The instruments of ratification shall be deposited with the Secretary-General of the Council of Europe, who will notify all Members of the names of those who have ratified.

In witness whereof, the undersigned, being duly authorised thereto, have signed this Protocol.

Done at Strasbourg, this 16th day of September 1963, in English and in French, both texts being equally authoritative, in a single copy which shall remain deposited in the archives of the Council of Europe. The Secretary-General shall transmit certified copies to each of the signatory States.

(Signed on behalf of the Governments of Austria, Belgium, Denmark, West Germany, Iceland, Ireland, Italy, Luxembourg, Netherlands, Norway, Sweden, and the United Kingdom.)

PROTOCOL No. 5 TO THE CONVENTION FOR THE PROTECTION OF HUMAN RIGHTS AND FUNDAMENTAL FREEDOMS,

amending Articles 22 and 40 of the Convention

The Governments signatory hereto, being Members of the Council of Europe,

Considering that certain inconveniences have arisen in the application of the provisions of Articles 22 and 40 of the Convention for the Protection of Human Rights and Fundamental Freedoms signed at Rome on 4th November 1950 (hereinafter referred to as 'the Convention') relating to the length of the terms of office of the members of the European Commission of Human Rights (hereinafter referred to as 'the Commission') and of the European Court of Human Rights (hereinafter referred to as 'the Court');

Considering that it is desirable to ensure as far as possible an election every three years of one half of the members of the Commission and of one third of the members of the Court;

Considering therefore that it is desirable to amend certain provisions of the Convention,

Have agreed as follows:

Article 1

In Article 22 of the Convention, the following two paragraphs shall be inserted after paragraph (2):

'(3) In order to ensure that, as far as possible, one half of the membership of the Commission shall be renewed every three years, the Committee of Ministers may decide, before proceeding to any subsequent election, that the term or terms of office of one or more members to be elected shall be for a period other than six years but not more than nine and not less than three years.

(4) In cases where more than one term of office is involved and the Committee of Ministers applies the preceding paragraph, the allocation of the terms of office shall be effected by

the drawing of lots by the Secretary-General, immediately after the election.'

Article 2

In Article 22 of the Convention, the former paragraphs (3) and (4) shall become respectively paragraphs (5) and (6).

Article 3

In Article 40 of the Convention, the following two paragraphs shall be inserted after paragraph (2):

'(3) In order to ensure that, as far as possible, one third of the membership of the Court shall be renewed every three years, the Consultative Assembly may decide, before proceeding to any subsequent election, that the term or terms of office of one or more members to be elected shall be for a period other than nine years but not more than twelve and not less than six years.

(4) In cases where more than one term of office is involved and the Consultative Assembly applies the preceding paragraph, the allocation of the terms of office shall be effected by the drawing of lots by the Secretary-General immediately after the election.'

Article 4

In Article 40 of the Convention, the former paragraphs (3) and (4) shall become respectively paragraphs (5) and (6).

Article 5

1. This Protocol shall be open to signature by Members of the Council of Europe, signatories to the Convention, who may become Parties to it by:

(*a*) signature without reservation in respect of ratification or acceptance;

(*b*) signature with reservation in respect of ratification or acceptance, followed by ratification or acceptance.

Instruments of ratification or acceptance shall be deposited with the Secretary-General of the Council of Europe.

2. This Protocol shall enter into force as soon as all Contracting Parties to the Convention shall have become Parties to the

Protocol, in accordance with the provisions of paragraph 1 of this Article.

3. The Secretary-General of the Council of Europe shall notify the Members of the Council of:

(a) any signature without reservation in respect of ratification or acceptance;

(b) any signature with reservation in respect of ratification or acceptance;

(c) the deposit of any instrument of ratification or acceptance;

(d) the date of entry into force of this Protocol in accordance with paragraph 2 of this Article.

In witness whereof the undersigned, being duly authorised thereto, have signed this Protocol.

Done at Strasbourg, this 20th day of January 1966, in English and in French, both texts being equally authoritative, in a single copy which shall remain deposited in the archives of the Council of Europe. The Secretary-General shall transmit certified copies to each of the signatory Governments.

(Signed on behalf of the Governments of Austria, Belgium, Cyprus, Denmark, West Germany, Iceland, Ireland, Italy, Luxembourg, Malta, Norway, Sweden, and the United Kingdom.)

Notes

Chapter 1

1. John Locke (1632–1704) wrote his *Letter on Toleration* (1689) and *Two Treatises of Government* (1690) some years before the 'Glorious Revolution' in England, but his writings provide the best theoretical justification for what was then accomplished.
2. *The Rights of Man*, London, 1944, p. 37.

Chapter 2

1. See A. P. d'Entrèves, *Natural Law*, London, 1951.
2. Edited by W. von Leyden, Oxford, 1952.
3. *The Concept of Mind*, London, 1949, p. 128.
4. Burke, *Works*, London, 1852, Vol. V, pp. 180–81.

Chapter 3

1. See G. Sartori, 'Constitutionalism', *American Political Science Review*, LVI, (December, 1962), pp. 853–65.

Chapter 5

1. Epictetus IV, I, 34.
2. Etymol. Magnum, 329, 44.
3. Max Pohlenz, *Freedom in Greek Life and Thought*, Dordrecht, Holland, 1966, p. 181.
4. As proclaimed in Article 15 (1) of the Universal Declaration: 'Everyone has the right to a nationality.'
5. Julius Isaac, *Economics of Migration*, London, 1947, p. 8.
6. M. Rostovtsev, *The Social and Economic History of the Roman Empire*, London, 1946.
7. C. Wirszubski, *Libertas*, Cambridge, 1952.
8. H. Pirenne, *Economic and Social History of Medieval Europe*, London, 1947, p. 52.
9. W. Petty, *A Treatise of Taxes and Contributions*, I, p. 34.
10. J. S. Mill, *On Liberty*, ed. H. B. Acton, London, 1972, p. 68.
11. Peter Reddaway, *Uncensored Russia*, London, 1972.

Chapter 6

1. 'Property I have nowhere found more clearly explained, than in a book entitled *Two Treatises of Government*', Locke to the Rev Richard King, August 25, 1703.

Chapter 7

1. H. Lauterpächt, *International Law and Human Rights*, London, 1951.
2. U.N. General Assembly Annexes (X), Agenda item 28 (Part II), p. 3.
3. U.N. General Assembly Records, Fifth Session, Resolution 421 (V) F (my italics).
4. U.N. Economic and Social Council, Vol. II (2), Special Supplement (supp. 5, para. 37).
5. 'The Ninth Session of the Commission on Human Rights held at Geneva from April 7 to May 30, 1953 . . . began with an announcement by the U.S. representative that our government did not intend to sign or ratify the draft *covenants* on Human Rights to which the Commission had devoted virtually its entire attention since 1948', *Bulletin of the Department of State*, Washington D.C., Vol. XXIX, 738, August 17, 1953.
6. General Assembly records, Annexes, Agenda item 28 (Part II), Tenth Session, pp. 81–2.
7. ibid.
8. *Annual Review of U.N. Affairs, 1970–1*, ed. by Florenz Remz, Dobbs Ferry, N.Y., 1972.
9. E. Soc. Resolution 1237, June 6, 1967.
10. With the notable exception of Communist China, which used its veto in the Security Council to deny Bangladesh membership of the United Nations in August 1972.
11. Both the United Kingdom and Greece made reservations with regard to this clause when they signed the Protocol.

Chapter 8

1. Arthur L. Corbin, introduction to W. N. Hohfeld's *Fundamental Legal Conceptions*, New Haven, 1964.
2. August 12, 1972.
3. Some two years before the episode in the Central African Republic, the then Secretary-General of the United Nations, U Thant, said in the introduction to his Annual Report: 'I feel it incumbent upon me to inform Member States of my deep concern regarding the persistent use of kidnappings, physical brutality and torture in many parts of the world. Such odious methods should be condemned and eradicated, whether they occur in time of peace or of armed conflict, whether they are inflicted by public authorities or by private individuals. It appears necessary once again to recall the solemn pledge contained in Article 5 of the Universal Declaration of Human Rights, and repeated in Article 7 of the International Covenant of Human Rights, that "no one shall be subjected to torture or to cruel, inhuman or degrading treatment or punishment". It is imperative for all States and groups to renounce such despicable practices and to demonstrate their avowed belief in respect for the integrity and dignity of all human beings.' *Annual Review of U.N. Affairs, 1969–70*, ed. B. A. Kulzer, Dobbs Ferry, N.Y., 1971.

Chapter 9

1. For text see *United Nations Yearbook* 1966, pp. 419 ff.
2. Quoted Radio Liberty Research, CRD/358/71
3. op. cit., p. 319.
4. Cornelia Mee, *The Internment of Soviet Dissenters in Mental Hospitals*, Cambridge, Mass., 1972.
5. *Annual Review of U.N. Affairs, 1967–8*, ed. by R. N. Swift, Dobbs Ferry, N.Y., 1969, p. 25. Professor Swift's preface to this annual review of United Nations affairs contains the melancholy reflection that the 'United Nations influence is small' in human rights questions (p. xi).
6. In the introduction to his last report as Secretary-General, U Thant said: '. . . I am concerned by the slowness in ratification of the International covenants on human rights, and I would urge an immediate acceleration of that process, because the coming into force of the Covenants will undoubtedly enhance the ability of the United Nations to protect human rights.' *Annual Review of U.N. Affairs, 1970–1*, ed. by Florence Remz, Dobbs Ferry, N.Y., 1972, p. 63.
7. U.N. General Assembly Records Annexes, Tenth Session (1955), Agenda item 28 (Part II), p. 48.
8. *The Concept of Law*, Oxford, 1961, pp. 205–6.
9. op. cit., p. 74.
10. Quoted by Peter Abrahams, 'L'Afrique et l'Occident', *Comprendre*, No. 13–14, Venice, 1955, p. 11.

Appendix C

1. Text amended in accordance with Article 1 of the Third Protocol to the Convention. The original text of Article 29 read as follows:
   '(1) The Commission shall perform the functions set out in Article 28 by means of a Sub-Commission consisting of 7 members of the Commission.
   (2) Each of the parties concerned may appoint as members of this Sub-Commission a person of its choice.
   (3) The remaining members shall be chosen by lot in accordance with arrangements prescribed in the Rules of Procedure of the Commission.'
2. Text amended in accordance with Article 2 of the Third Protocol to the Convention. The original text of Article 30 commenced with the words 'If the Sub-Commission succeeds . . .'.
3. Text amended in accordance with Article 3 of the Third Protocol to the Convention. The original text of Article 34 read as follows:
   'The Commission shall take its decisions by a majority of the members present and voting; the Sub-Commission shall take its decision by a majority of its members.'
4. The words 'signatories to the Convention' did not appear in the original English text of Article 4. This technical error was corrected by a certificate of correction of the Secretary-General of April 14, 1967.
5. Greece ceased, on June 13, 1970, to be a Party to the European Convention on Human Rights.

DATE DUE

NOV 12 '85			
NOV 26 '85			
APR 0 8 2004			